RTI Strategies That Work in the 3–6 Classroom

T0383063

Eli Johnson
and
Michelle Karns

EYE ON EDUCATION
6 DEPOT WAY WEST, SUITE 106
LARCHMONT, NY 10538
(914) 833–0551
(914) 833–0761 fax
www.eyeoneducation.com

A sincere effort has been made to supply the identity of those who have created specific strategies. Any omissions have been unintentional.

Library of Congress Cataloging-in-Publication Data

Johnson, Eli R.
 RTI strategies that work in the 3-6 classroom / Eli Johnson and
Michelle Karns.
    p. cm.
 ISBN 978-1-59667-213-0
1. Remedial teaching. 2. Response to intervention (Learning
disabled children) 3. Language arts (Elementary) 4. Mathematics—
Study and teaching (Elementary) I. Karns, Michelle. II. Title.
 LB1029.R4J633 2011
 371.9--dc23

                                                          2011049127

Sponsoring Editor: Robert Sickles
Production Editor: Lauren Davis
Copyeditor: Elayne Masters
Designer and Compositor: Rick Soldin
Cover Designer: Knoll Gilbert

Also Available from Eye On Education

RTI Strategies That Work in the K–2 Classroom
Eli Johnson and Michelle Karns

Questions and Answers About RTI:
A Guide to Success
Heather Moran and Anthony Petruzzelli

RTI and CSI:
Using Data, Vision, and Leadership to Design, Implement,
and Evaluate a Schoolwide Prevention System
Victoria L. Bernhardt and Connie L. Hébert

Improving Adolescent Literacy:
An RTI Implementation Guide
Pamela S. Craig and Rebecca K. Sarlo

Transforming High Schools Through Response to Intervention:
Lessons Learned and a Pathway Forward
Jeremy Koselak

Active Literacy Across the Curriculum
Heidi Hayes Jacobs

Motivating Every Student in Literacy
(Including the Highly Unmotivated!), Grades 3–6
Sandra Athans and Denise Ashe Devine

Awakening Brilliance in the Writer's Workshop:
Using Notebooks, Mentor Texts, and the Writing Process
Lisa Morris

Writer's Workshop for the Common Core:
A Step-by-Step Guide
Warren E. Combs

Literacy from A to Z
Barbara R. Blackburn

Contents

Free Downloads

Several of the resources discussed and displayed in this book are also available on Eye On Education's Web site as Adobe Acrobat files. Permission has been granted to purchasers of this book to download these resources and print them.

You can access these downloads by visiting Eye On Education's Web site: www.eyeoneducation.com. From the home page, click on FREE, then click on Supplemental Downloads. Alternatively, you can search or browse our Web site to find this book, then click on "Log in to Access Supplemental Downloads."

Your book-buyer access code is RTI-7-213-0.

Index of Free Downloads

RTI Strategies That Work in the 3–6 Classroom
Strategy Matrix

Listening Intervention Strategies	Page Number
Root Words	29
Brick and Mortar Words	38
Academic Language Graphic Organizer	44
Purposeful Prepositions	49
Figures of Speech	56
Reading Intervention Strategies	
Guided Reading	65
Comparing Text Structures	69
Content Inferences	74
Signal Words	78
Thinking Aloud	82
Math Intervention Strategies	
Questioning Aloud	89
Estimating Conversations	94
Fabulous Fractions	99
Measurement/Geometry Shapes	102
Algebra Fundamentals	107
Speaking Intervention Strategies	
Informational Storytelling	116
Structured Group Discussions	119
Language Code-Switching	124
Jigsaw Conversations	129
Academic Content Talk	131
Writing Intervention Strategies	
Writing Aloud	142
Paragraph-Style Writing	147
Opinion-Based Writing	151
Narrative Story Structure	155
Informative/Explanatory Writing Structure	162

About the Authors

Eli Johnson is currently Chief Academic Officer for a rural district in the Central Valley of California. He provides trainings for school districts and regional organizations throughout the United States. He has previously served as an educational consultant for the California Department of Education, Assistant Superintendent of Curriculum and Instruction, High School Principal, Assistant Principal, and classroom teacher. His schools have made the highest annual point gains in the state of California and have been awarded the U.S. News & World Report Medal Honors. Eli received his undergraduate degree in education from Brigham Young University (Go Cougars!) and his graduate degree in education from the University of Washington (Go Huskies!). He is the author of *Academic Language! Academic Literacy!* and co-author of *RTI Strategies That Work in the K–2 Classroom*. Eli is married to his wonderful wife Shaunna, and they are the parents of five children: Natalie, Mikaila, Bryce, Erica, and Benjamin.

Michelle Karns is an educational consultant with more than 30 years of experience working with struggling learners and students impacted by adversity. She strives to develop remedies to answer their individual learning, instructional, organizational, and community needs. Michelle is committed to the realization of successful outcomes for every child. She has the unique ability to translate complex theory into easy-to-use, meaningful techniques and applications for classroom settings. Working with students, administrators, and teachers in districts throughout the United States and Canada, Michelle helps create the conditions for all students to learn and make academic success a reality. An author of several books and multiple educational reform articles for the Association of California School Administrator's *Leadership Magazine*, she has helped thousands of students and teachers build positive relationships and meet their academic and personal success goals.

Preface

The number one issue we face in American education is meeting the academic needs of all of our students. We have accomplished much in the areas of curriculum, instruction, assessment, and many other aspects of learning. All of these efforts have highlighted the need for so many of our students to receive intervention support to ensure their academic success. Teachers all over the nation have excitedly clamored for clear and concise resource guides to support their struggling students.

As a result of this growing interest in classroom interventions, a model for what is commonly called Response to Intervention (RTI) has come to the forefront of education. Response to Intervention has been adopted by the federal government, several states, and many districts throughout the country. Numerous books address the challenges with implementing a RTI model in a school or school district. This book is different in that it provides powerful and practical strategies specifically for classroom teachers, academic coaches, instructional aides, and support specialists. The chapters provide intervention strategies that will help students in grades 3–6 develop the listening, reading, mathematics, speaking, and writing skills they need. Each chapter connects the Common Core State Standards to the interventions students need to help them meet these standards.

As educational consultants, we have worked with a variety of teachers at different grade levels who have attended our RTI Strategies That Work workshops and trainings. Out of these workshops came a clear request for RTI strategies that are effective with various grade levels. *RTI Strategies That Work in the 3–6 Classroom* is the second book in a series of books that meets this need. You may already be familiar with the first book: *RTI Strategies That Work in the K–2 Classroom*, also published by Eye On Education. Each book offers RTI strategies with step-by-step examples that help students learn.

All of the strategies in this current volume are specifically proven to work for students in grades 3–6. You can read this book sequentially from front to back, or you can jump from chapter to the chapter and target the strategies that will provide the greatest benefit to your students. However you choose to use this classroom resource, please enjoy each of the RTI strategies. We look forward to hearing about your students' progress.

Sincerely,
Eli Johnson & Michelle Karns

1

Classroom Intervention Strategies That Work

"It is the supreme art of the teacher
to awaken joy in creative expression and knowledge."

—Albert Einstein

Sierra entered fourth grade already behind in school. She missed many days in third grade, and school has always felt like a blur of people, activities, and transitions. She hopelessly grapples with her classwork and struggles with her homework and rarely has any success. Sierra is on track to drop out of school by tenth grade and become another educational casualty. Statistics say that she has a 70 percent chance of making it through high school. Her parents both work hard in the fields to provide for Sierra and her eight siblings. She gets very little individual attention from anyone. Her parents love her dearly, but they have no capacity to help Sierra. Why? They never got past the fourth grade—the same grade she's in right now. Without a targeted intervention that meets her individual needs, she will continue to struggle, eventually dropping out without any economic opportunities and becoming another statistic.

Many students in our schools face the same challenges Sierra faces. They often sit quietly on the sidelines of learning and never really engage in school. They lack many of the essential skills to succeed in school and have no way to learn them. Each year they get further and further behind until the cumulative effect reveals glaring gaps in their skills, strategies, and abilities as learners. Without effective classroom instruction and specialized interventions, these students will face many more difficult challenges in the years to come, affecting the rest of their lives. Irvin, Meltzer, & Dukes (2007) state that "interventions provide students with the tools and strategies they need to make great strides in literacy development" (p. 268).

The overall statistics of student struggles are disturbing, and the individual stories can be heart-wrenching. We need to equip our students with the strategies that will help them change the trajectory of their future.

Academic Dropouts

According to the 2004 Dropout Prevention Act, there are many characteristics indicative of potential problems leading to a dropout decision: poor attendance, low grade point average, low standardized test scores, special program placement, grade retention, discipline referrals and suspensions, mobility, teen parenthood, and below-average math and reading ability (USDE, 2004). Sparks & Johnson found that there are three significant factors that are consistent with dropping out: 1) being retained in any grade, 2) receiving long-term suspensions, and 3) scoring below grade level in reading and math (ASCD, 2010). The factors that contribute to this dropout phenomenon are linked to high mobility, lack of literate role models, and chaotic lifestyles.

However, there are many children living in socioeconomic conditions that are indicative of poverty who function well in schools. What are the differences? Adults who are invested in intervening academically on behalf of the child (Benard, 2004). If we consistently implement strategies that focus on instructional goals, provide meaningful learning activities, and show our care and concern for their success, our struggling students will be empowered to overcome adversity.

Dilemmas with Diversity

We face an important turning point in American education. In our schools and classrooms, educators are asked to teach a continually increasing population of diverse students. We work with students who have greater diversity in race, language, culture, and background than ever before. As we work to make sure every student learns at grade level, the diversity dynamic brings some very significant challenges. The needs for each student are becoming less common. Pretending that education is a one-size-fits-all model will have disastrous results in the future. More and more students have diverse educational experiences, cognitive abilities, economic resources, and emotional support. Peter S. Jennison (1998) highlights the disparity between the language skills of poor students and affluent students.

> The poor and the affluent are not communicating because they do not have the same words. When we talk of the millions who are culturally deprived, we refer not to those who do not have access to good libraries and bookstores, or to museums and centers for the performing arts, but those deprived of the words with which everything else is built, the words that open doors. Children without words are licked before they start. The legion of the young wordless in urban and rural slums, eight to ten years old, do not know the meaning of hundreds of words which most middle-class people assume to be familiar to much younger children.

Minorities and children of poverty top the list of students who are two or more years behind grade level. These challenges highlight our need for powerful core instruction supported by interventions that will address the wide variety of students in our classrooms. The clear overidentification of certain demographic groups in special services indicates a bias (Harry & Klingner, 2006). More and more affected students are now being inclusively added to regular grade-level classrooms. Special Education traditionally followed a discrepancy model which determined that once a student became several grade levels behind, the student would be placed in Special Education. This is a "wait to fail" model. We need one that proactively addresses concerns when they first arise. The discrepancy model lacks the specific instructional approaches our students need as individuals to make progress towards success.

Instruction and Intervention

We need to get to the core issue of education, which is the quality of instruction. Rather than attempting to hack at the leaves of education, this book gets right down to the root of the matter. The quality of education hinges on the quality of overall instruction (Marzano et al, 2001) as well as the targeted interventions that address students' differentiated learning styles. Many teachers develop only a limited number of strategies in their instructional repertoire to meet the needs of their students (Karen E. Johnson, 2008). It is one thing to be aware that an intervention is needed. It is another to put the necessary structure in place that addresses the learning needs. Webster & Fisher (2001) note that

Teachers and the instructional approaches they use are fundamental in building students' understanding. Primary among
their many duties and responsibilities, teachers structure and
guide the pace of individual, small-group and whole-class
work to present new material, engage students in learning
tasks, and help deepen students' grasp of the content and
concepts being studied. (p. 2)

We have so many students who feel that they need support to help them
reach their educational potential. It is crucial that the instructional capacity is
in place to meet their personal learning needs.

Who Needs Classroom Intervention Strategies?

Every teacher in America will benefit from intervention strategies that
meet the needs of their students. Teachers consistently are on the look-out for
classroom strategies that will reach and help even the most challenging student. For example, as we (the authors) interact with teachers and administrators at workshops across the county, the number one concern we consistently
hear is "I need intervention strategies that I can do in my classroom to meet the
needs of my struggling students." Also, one first-year teacher asked, "What
do I do with my students who have a variety of issues related to poverty?" An
elementary principal shared, "At my school many of our students are more
than one grade level behind in reading." An experienced teacher mentioned,
"My English Language Learners often seem lost in my classroom." While
many students from a variety of circumstances may need intervention, the
research shows that students in three particular areas (Figure 1.1) definitely
need classroom intervention strategies to help them develop as learners.

Figure 1.1 Children Most in Need of Instructional Intervention Strategies

1. Children raised in poverty
2. Children who are English Language Learners
3. Children who struggle with phonological processing, memory difficul-
    ties, speech or hearing impairments

(Honig, Diamond, & Gutlohn, 2000, p. 13)

In the past, these low socioeconomic students, English Language Learners, and struggling readers may have been assigned to special classes. Under RTI, many of these students are now expected to succeed within the regular classroom. Let's look at some of the specific needs of these students.

Low Socioeconomic Students (Title I)

Children are adversely affected by the challenges of low socio-economic circumstances. Students from low socioeconomic backgrounds typically lack a myriad of resources that affect their results in school. Like Sierra, whom we introduced at the beginning of this chapter, these students need targeted intervention strategies that will help them develop their knowledge and understanding. Without early school interventions, these students face falling behind their grade-level peers, dropping out of school altogether, and being at risk for a host of other unfortunate life events (Stone, Silliman, Ehren, & Appel, 2005).

English Language Learners (ELLs)

Our 3–6 classrooms are filling up with increasing numbers of English Language Learners. Again, these students need specific, targeted interventions to overcome the effects of learning a new language. Approximately 50 percent of English Language Learners drop out of school (Alliance for Excellent Education, 2009). It's not unusual for ELL students to speak their native language in the home, so school may be the only place where many ELL students have a chance to hear and produce language in English. These students need strategies that will help them deal with the challenges of learning a second language. Our ELL students need *classroom intervention strategies that work*, and they need these strategies so they can develop the language skills required to succeed in school.

Struggling Readers (Special Needs)

Struggling readers come to school in many shapes and sizes. Like Sierra, struggling readers find school extremely challenging. With so much learning conveyed through classroom texts and stories, difficulty with reading significantly influences learning. It can be tough to spot these students by just looking at them, yet when they open a book and begin reading out loud, the issues present themselves quite readily. Research shows that unless high-need students receive targeted interventions, many will face increasing gaps in their learning and achievement (Rathvon, 2008). If no interventions are provided at an early age, many of these students may be destined for special education classrooms. Struggling readers and low socioeconomic students need *intervention strategies that work*, and they need them early and often.

Low socioeconomic students, English Language Learners, and struggling readers need consistent classroom interventions. Without this additional support, our neediest students will continue to struggle in school.

RTI Strategies Matter

The RTI model provides a framework for outlining who is responsible in schools for initial instructional support for those students who struggle to keep up with grade-level standards. Most books on RTI neglect to note that the classroom teacher is the key to making RTI work. Typical explanations of the RTI model do little to outline how teachers and support staff are to use research-based intervention strategies to target the specific needs of students. The number one question that teachers so often ask us is "How do I provide effective intervention strategies that will work and help all students learn proficiently at grade level?" Interventions help us achieve success in our classrooms for our individual students and our collective nation. Ramey & Ramey (1998) emphasize that students need to be provided strategies that prime the development of learning in several ways:

- ◆ Mentoring in basic cognitive skills and strategies

- ◆ Encouragement of concept exploration

- ◆ Celebrating new skills and strategies

- ◆ Stimulation in language and symbolic communication

- ◆ Guided rehearsal and extension of new skills and strategies (p. 115)

Third- through sixth-grade teachers want to know, "What should I do when I first begin to see my students falling behind?" While the myriad of issues our students bring to the table are extensive, there are some targeted intervention strategies that will support students with learning challenges.

The interventions need to start early. Waiting for issues to resolve themselves without targeted help only puts children on a treadmill of repeated failure. Making sure that all children have preschool experiences is a systemic intervention worthy of consideration and support. Intervention strategies should be provided as soon as learning problems become evident.

What Does a Response to Intervention (RTI) Model Look Like?

Let's take some time to see what a Response to Intervention (RTI) model of instruction looks like. RTI has become the national model for addressing struggling students' needs (United States Department of Education, 2009). Many states, such as New York and Iowa, have already passed legislation that makes RTI the official educational response for our schools. Let's begin by looking at definitions of *response*, *intervention*, and *strategy* from Dictionary.com (2010):

Response
1. An answer or reply to a situation.
2. A chosen course of action that addresses a specific issue.

Intervention
1. An interference that redirects the current path an individual is on.
2. Actions that produce a positive change in results and outcomes.

The RTI process typically follows a three-tier (Tier I, Tier II, & Tier III) model that begins with a focus on interventions in the classroom (Bernhardt & Hebert, 2011).

Effective classroom interventions are designed to meet the needs of 80 percent of the students. For students who need additional strategic interventions, more time should be spent in targeted small-group instruction (four to six students), which should meet the needs of an additional 15 percent of students. Even with this level of intervention, some students will struggle to meet grade-level standards. Interventions that provide intensive support are necessary to reach the remaining five percent. In Figure 1.2 at the top of the next page, the shaded sections identify three different levels of interventions:

Tier I: Classroom Interventions are designed for all students, and they should reach approximately 80 percent of students.

Figure 1.2 Three-Tiered Response to Intervention (RTI) Model

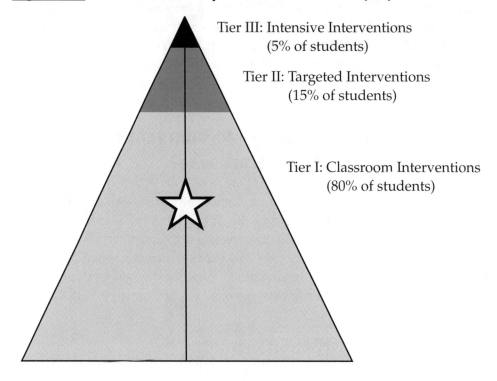

Tier III: Intensive Interventions
(5% of students)

Tier II: Targeted Interventions
(15% of students)

Tier I: Classroom Interventions
(80% of students)

These are universal interventions that are proactive, preventive, and differentiated and may be delivered through whole-group or small-group instruction.

Tier II: Strategic Interventions should help some students, an additional 15 percent of students. These targeted interventions for at-risk students involve frequent checking and assessing of progress.

Tier III: Intensive Interventions should support a few students, the final five percent of students. These are extremely focused interventions that may involve as few as one or two students at a time who receive instruction that is specifically suited to their specific needs. Interventions at Tier III are most often delivered by specialists while school psychologists provide regular assessment feedback.

As you can see from Figure 1.2, the most important interventions that reach the greatest number of students are high-quality classroom interventions.

Figure 1.3 RTI Matrix

RTI Tier	Intervention Level	Targeted Students	Best Practices	Expected Results
Tier I	Classroom Intervention	All Students	◆ Universal screening ◆ Research-based practices ◆ Explicit instruction ◆ Consistent progress monitoring	80% of students at grade level
Tier II	Targeted Intervention	Some Students	◆ More time ◆ More attention ◆ Increased support ◆ Targeted progress monitoring	15% of students at grade level
Tier III	Intensive Intervention	A Few Students	◆ Individualized instruction ◆ Individualized assessment based on student needs	5% of students at grade level

Students who continue to struggle may be given interventions that target specific student needs. Finally, students who continue to struggle should be provided intensive interventions. The majority of the strategies in this book are Tier I and Tier II interventions designed to keep students in grades 3–6 on grade level. Figure 1.3 shows best practices for each tier.

Students who show repeated signs of difficulty grasping strategies or have Tier III needs should be referred to a special education specialist or school psychologist who can provide more extensive assessments and support.

Cracks, Gaps, and Chasms

The achievement gap and the growing dropout rate reveal the significant challenges many of our students face. Many English Language Learners and students of color are two or more years behind their grade-level peers. Our students definitely need interventions that work and that address these concerns. So what is the root cause behind these issues that affect so many of our students? Ed Hirsch (2003) points out, "It is now well accepted that

Figure 1.4 Cracks, Gaps, and Chasms

Language Cracks: Cracks begin to show up in the learning foundation as students enter school.

Literacy Gaps: Over time, gaps begin to appear in the framework that holds learning together.

Learning Chasms: Eventually, chasms begin engulfing large groups of students (especially the poor, minorities, and struggling readers), who then face growing dropout rates.

the chief cause of the achievement gap between socioeconomic groups is a language gap" (p. 22). Cracks in the foundation of students' language can appear before students even enter kindergarten. If these cracks in students' language foundation are ignored, they often widen over time. Eventually, they can lead to gaps in literacy and can eventually overwhelm our students' ability to learn (see Figure 1.4). Simply stated, the language cracks that appear in the early elementary grades become significant literacy gaps in the upper elementary grades. In time, as students transition from middle school to high school, learning chasms begin to appear that swallow up entire groups of English Language Learners, socioeconomically disadvantaged students, and struggling readers.

Unless the cracks are systematically addressed using targeted interventions, the cracks will become gaps and eventually chasms. For example, one of the authors served as an administrator at an inner-city high school in a large metropolitan area. The school had eight hundred freshmen enter the campus each year. Four years later, the school graduated approximately 400 seniors, evidence of a 50 percent dropout rate. *What happened to these students? Where did they go?* They slipped into the cracks, got wedged into the gaps, and eventually fell into the chasms of our educational system. The language cracks that start to appear in elementary grades become literacy gaps by the time many of these students reach middle school, and by the time these students reach high school, the cracks and gaps develop into learning chasms. These chasms are swallowing entire groups of students, and these students are dropping out in monumental numbers.

Kids seem better able to succeed with the language and learning of the streets than with the language and learning of school. Is it any wonder that so many of our students are dropping out in such large numbers? We need effective strategies that work to fill the cracks, gaps, and chasms that show up in our students' learning.

Creating Knowledge Structures

In order to target the cracks, gaps, and chasms that may become a reality for our students, we need to understand the critical elements of language, literacy, and learning that affect our students. A crucial part of a high-quality intervention program is recognizing the key components of how we create knowledge structures or structure our learning. A primary purpose of educational interventions is to create knowledge structures that help students build a house of learning (Figure 1.5). It is exciting to see students who have developed stable structures of knowledge that solidify their current learning. A primary purpose of educational interventions is to create knowledge structures and help students build a house of learning and establish a basis for future learning. To design effective interventions, we must understand the vital role of language, literacy, and learning.

Figure 1.5 House of Knowledge Structures

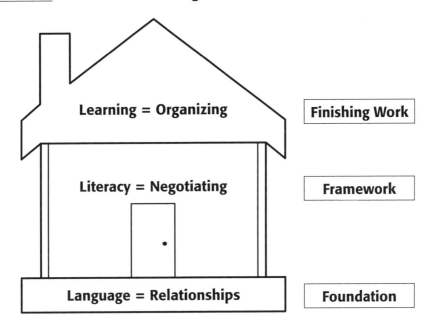

Language Is the Foundation

Interventions need to start with language, since language is the basic building block or chief component of constructing knowledge (Kamil & Pearson, 2007). So what is the key role of language in developing learning? Language creates the relationships between letters, sounds, words, definitions, sentences, and meaning. Students who have cracks in their language relationships struggle to become literate learners.

Language = Relationships

Without language, it is difficult for relationships to develop. In the Bible story about the Tower of Babel, when people lost the ability to communicate, their relationships were affected. Consider the following examples of how language affects learning relationships.

Academic Foundation

1. Sound = Symbol relationship
2. Blending = Decoding relationship
3. Word = Meaning relationship
4. Background Knowledge = Current connection relationship
5. Word = Picture relationship
6. Academic Language = Access learning relationship
7. Word = Sentence relationship
8. Casual Language = Academic language relationship

As our students learn the fundamental relationships between sounds and symbols, words and meaning, prior knowledge and new connections, and language and learning, they will develop the skills needed to succeed in school.

Literacy Is the Framework

Once students have a firm foundation in language, interventions should focus on creating a sound framework. Literacy is the next step in building stable knowledge structures that contribute to a house of learning. Literacy is an interesting concept. Skills like fluency and comprehension contribute to developing a robust literacy framework. Literacy bridges the gap between language skills and learning strategies. So what exactly is literacy all about? In a nutshell, literacy is about developing the skills to effectively negotiate the principles of language and the demands of learning.

Literacy = Negotiating

At first glance this may seem like an interesting pairing. Yet, as you think about it, becoming literate is a process of negotiating. Bearne, Dombey, and Grainger (2003) note that "negotiating meaning and making sense are basic to all literate behavior" (p. 158). Reading is a process in which a reader negotiates meaning with the author of the book through language. When young readers engage with a book they are in fact negotiating meaning with the author. Other words that correspond to literacy are interaction or transaction. We develop literacy when we interact with others through language and negotiate or transact an exchange of knowledge. Literate individuals are good readers, listeners, speakers, and writers. They use language to communicate effectively and efficiently with others. Consider the following examples of how literacy helps us negotiate learning.

Academic Framework

1. Reader = Author negotiation
2. Cognitive Processing = Meaning interaction
3. Writer = Audience negotiation
4. Listener = Interpreting active exchange
5. Speaker = Audience active exchange
6. Connecting = Inferring cognition
7. Inquiry = Insight connections
8. Language Production = Process language connections

Our students need to negotiate the demands of learning or interact efficiently with others to transmit and process knowledge. For example, listening and reading are processes for negotiating meaning with a speaker or author, and speaking and writing are processes for negotiating meaning with an audience. As our students learn to transact knowledge fluently and with automaticity, they will be able to learn much more rapidly.

Learning Is the Finishing Work

Once students have the skills of language and the automaticity of literacy, they can really focus on the finishing work of learning. Language gives students a firm foundation to build their house of knowledge. Literacy gives students a stable framework for constructing their house of knowledge. And ultimately, learning allows students to do the finishing work on their house of knowledge. The finishing work allows us to organize information into knowledge. Finishing work determines where we place a door or window, what color we paint the walls, and how we decorate the interior parts of our house of knowledge. At its core, learning is all about the ability to organize information into knowledge that we can remember and retrieve when we need to access it.

Learning = Organizing

Students who have both a firm foundation of language and a stable framework of literacy and can do the finishing work of learning will be able to confidently take hold of their lives and future. Consider the following examples of how learning is the finishing work that helps us organize knowledge.

Academic Finishing Work

1. Compare/Contrast
2. Cause/Effect
3. Problem/Solution
4. Chronological Sequence
5. Description
6. Classification/Categorization
7. Hierarchy of Knowledge
8. Knowledge Structures

For our students to become lifelong learners, they must have the ability to connect learning relationships, negotiate literacy demands, and organize knowledge in sustainable structures that will benefit them for years to come.

Effective Intervention Grouping

Targeted classroom interventions should be started early and used often. Students need intervention supports provided to them the same day that they struggle to grasp objectives and skills. Each day, teachers should devote time to working with a small group of four to six students who need additional support mastering the skills and objectives outlined in the daily lesson. The earlier students receive intervention strategies, the sooner they will be able to produce results. A quality RTI program begins in the classroom. The classroom teacher is best positioned to see concerns and address them right away. Let's look at three areas of focus that the classroom teacher needs to master in order to provide effective intervention strategies:

Whole Class Intervention: Interventions at this level are provided by classroom teachers to support the core instruction for all students and are designed to meet the needs of at least 80 percent of the students. Effective teachers recognize where struggling students are falling through cracks and gaps in learning, and they provide classroom intervention strategies to meet the needs of those students.

Targeted Small Group Intervention: The teacher will invite a group of four to six students to the small group instruction (peapod) table to receive more time and attention on intervention strategies that will help students achieve necessary knowledge, skills, and objectives. Targeted small group instruction typically requires teachers to devote 30 minutes to ensure that struggling students have sufficiently learned the daily objectives. (The next section in this chapter will discuss core components of classroom intervention strategies that work.)

Independent Practice: While the teacher is focused on small group intervention, the rest of the students in the class complete daily activities that allow students to practice the skills taught in the core lesson. Teachers can provide students with activities in two categories:

- ♦ **Must Dos**: Activities selected by the teacher to reinforce the lesson and provide students with independent practice.

- ♦ **May Dos**: Once students have completed all Must Do activities, they can then do the May Dos to extend and enhance their learning. This keeps advanced learners busy while the teacher provides struggling students with small group interventions.

The teacher writes on the board the daily Must Dos and May Dos that will help the bulk of the class (80 percent) demonstrate their mastery of the grade-level skills and objectives. Typically a teacher assigns one or two Must Dos and provides one or two May Dos that students can work on independently; the teacher can use this independent work time to concentrate more time and attention on struggling students.

Carving out additional time to focus on needy students is crucial. Always ask yourself, "Is this child performing within the range of grade-level expectations? If not, which strategies will make a difference?" Every classroom needs quality whole-group instruction and small-group interventions within the regular classroom. Our students need intervention strategies each and every day to help them accelerate their learning. Small-group interventions provide students with two important resources:

- ♦ **More Attention:** Small-group instruction focused on strategies; fewer students means more attention from the teacher.

- ♦ **More Time:** Additional time working with students on key intervention strategies.

As struggling students receive more attention and more time, more students will be able to achieve grade-level standards and expectations (Nobre & Coull, 2010). Highly successful schools and highly successful teachers provide their students with targeted intervention strategies that help each student achieve classroom success.

Core Competencies for Classroom Intervention Strategies That Work

Whether we are administrators, teachers, or instructional coaches, we first need to develop our own understanding of intervention strategies that work for students. We need in our instructional toolbox a repertoire of strategies that will achieve effective results. This instruction needs to have built-in interventions that address the varying needs of students. Our students in grades 3–6 need specific intervention strategies that will develop their ability in reading, writing, numeracy, listening, and speaking.

Core Intervention Competencies

- ♦ **Listening:** Strategies that help students focus and understand better

- ♦ **Reading:** Strategies that help students comprehend and handle text

- ♦ **Numeracy:** Strategies that help students compute and solve equations

- ♦ **Speaking:** Strategies that help students dialogue and engage with peers

- ♦ **Writing:** Strategies that help students compose and construct ideas

Our instructional arrows must hit the mark for the desired outcomes. And we need a variety of intervention strategies in our instructional quiver so that we can hit the mark and meet the different needs of our students.

What Do Intervention Strategies That Work Look Like?

Most Response to Intervention (RTI) frameworks offer few specific intervention strategies and as a result they do very little to advance student learning. A typical RTI workshop or training addresses how to assess kids or shift them around the school campus. It does very little as far as outlining how instruction should change for those students who need the most help. The top challenge right now in education is that classroom teachers lack familiarity with many of the targeted intervention strategies that will produce the desired results for struggling students. Targeted intervention strategies are used by effective teachers to meet the instructional needs of students. While there are many things that meet the needs of students, the four areas shown below are crucial to designing effective interventions.

Characteristics of High-Quality Tier I Intervention Strategies

1. **Access** (Language Support)
2. **Engagement** (Interactive and Internal Processing)
3. **Structure** (Knowledge Foundations and Cognitive Support)
4. **Meaning** (Pulling It All Together)

As we provide interventions that are specifically designed to support access to learning, student engagement, structured activities, and integration of meaning, our students will increase their academic achievement. RTI interventions need to start much earlier for students who need help. The classroom is the primary place interventions should occur. Let's look at each of these four keys to successful Tier I interventions.

Providing Access (Language Support)

The number one reason that the vast majority of our students are unable to succeed in school is their difficulty accessing the knowledge provided at school (Stone, Silliman, & Ehren, 2005). Access is difficult for many students because they lack the academic language and background knowledge needed to successfully access the learning provided in teachers' instruction and classroom textbooks. Brown-Chidsey, Bronaugh, & McGraw (2007) note it is essential that "each child has access to quality instruction and that struggling students—including those with learning disabilities—are identified early and receive the necessary support to be successful" (p. 16). Accessing learning through language is essential for success. Language provides the

Figure 1.6 Academic Language

Language Register	Number of Years Needed to Learn
Casual Language	1 to 2 years
Academic Language	5 to 7 years

ability to access learning. Students need access to learning through high-quality interventions that support language and learning (Shores & Chester, 2008). At the same time, a lack of language can limit students' ability to learn in school. The most important type of language at school is academic language. While it typically takes an English Language Learner one to two years to learn the casual language needed to talk in the neighborhood, on the playground, or with a classroom peer, it takes much longer for students to learn academic language (Figure 1.6). The reality is that many students never learn the academic language necessary to succeed in school (Johnson, 2009).

Even though English Language Learners can learn the academic language in 5 to 7 years, without targeted interventions many students never learn academic language and continue to struggle throughout school. Increasing student access to learning through strategies focused on language builds student progress (Maanum, 2009). Now let's look at a framework for

Figure 1.7 Framework for Reading

DECODING Learning to Read			COMPREHENSION Reading to Learn		
Word Recognition Strategies		Fluency	Academic Language		Comprehension Strategies
Concepts of Print · Phonemic Awareness · Phonics · Sight Words		Automaticity	Background Knowledge · Brick and Mortar Vocabulary · Syntax and Text Structure		Comprehension Monitoring · (Re)organizing Text

Adapted from John Shefelbine/Developmental Studies Center

developing reading from John Shefelbine outlined in the *Reading/Language Arts Framework for California Public Schools* (2007) (Figure 1.7). Note how academic language is essential in helping students transition from decoding (learning to read) to comprehension (reading to learn).

Students from poverty, English Language Learners, and struggling readers all have difficulty accessing learning because they lack the background knowledge and essential language that leads to effective learning.

Providing Engagement (Interactive and Internal Processing)

Students need interventions that are engaging and use all of the senses. Effective interventions are kinesthetically engaging, auditorily resonating, and visually stimulating. There is a direct correlation between engagement and academic achievement, particularly for students from poverty (Jon Douglas Wilms, 2003). The most powerful models of instruction are interactive. Instruction actively engages the learner and is generative. Instruction encourages the learner to construct and produce knowledge in meaningful ways. Students teach others interactively and interact generatively with their teacher and peers. This allows for co-construction of knowledge, which promotes engaged learning that is problem-, project-, and goal-based. Ivey & Fisher (2006) state that "it is easy to spot engaging instruction within an intervention. Students are eager to read and write" (p. 81).

Some common strategies of engaged-learning models of instruction include individual and group summarizing, means of exploring multiple perspectives, and techniques for building upon prior knowledge. Great intervention strategies are

- ♦ **Engaging**: Instruction and interventions that are engaging help students find excitement in learning. They become intrinsically motivated.

- ♦ **Interactive**: Students learn to work collaboratively and connect with their fellow classmates as they learn.

- ♦ **Energizing**: Effective strategies build energy and help students maintain their focus as they accelerate their learning.

In addition to engaging the external senses, effective interventions also engage internal learning processes. Most importantly, our students need to be internally engaged in extending, expanding, and elaborating on their learning. Reflecting on instruction and monitoring progress help students engage internally and identify learning successes and areas that require additional attention.

Providing Structure (Knowledge Foundations and Support)

Intervention strategies need to scaffold or provide workable chunks that students can grasp as they learn processes. Explicit instruction means that the students can see the specific steps needed to accomplish a task. Riccomini & Witzel (2009) emphasize that "the organization of RTI rests on a tiered system to structure instruction and interventions based on student needs" (p. 39). Students need frequent feedback along the way to make sure that they are on track. Students need learning processes modeled for them. In particular, the metacognitive processes that signify great learning—like summarizing, understanding, and making connections—provide the structures that strengthen and build learning. These processes and many others need to be clearly outlined in specific instructional steps that will help students learn and comprehend new information. As we jump into the five, upcoming chapters that outline the key strategies, you will notice that specific steps are provided for each strategy.

Providing Meaning (Pulling It All Together)

The ultimate objective of any lesson is for students to make meaning of the information they are learning. As Fullan (2001) insightfully says, "Acquiring meaning, of course, is an individual act but its real value for student learning is when shared meaning is achieved across a group of people working in concert" (p. 46). Many students go through lessons in class without really developing any meaningful learning. When students lack the academic language and academic literacy, quality classroom interventions can help students negotiate with the text, with their peers, and with their own sense of meaning. It is through the processes of negotiation with others that we develop greater literacy skills and gain insight into new learning experiences. Learning is a process of exchange where our students negotiate with their own understanding so they are able to make meaning. Interventions should encourage students to negotiate meaning with their teachers, classmates, and the authors of classroom texts.

Intervention Strategies That Work

We have many students who need us to respond to their intervention needs. In Chapters 2–6, we will look at classroom interventions that teachers can add to their toolbox of strategies. As we expand our instructional repertoire, we will be able to meet the needs of all our students. In the upcoming chapters, we will spell out twenty-five (25) intervention strategies that will support Tier I and Tier II RTI instruction with the whole classroom or small groups of students. Each chapter follows an easy-to-use format that provides background information, including the research behind the strategy, and details about what the strategy looks like, how the strategy works, why the strategy works, and how to monitor progress. In addition, a special boxed feature connecting the intervention strategies to the Common Core State Standards is provided. Also, a boxed feature on English Language Learners is provided to extend additional help to those students who need increased language support. Here is a brief overview of the chapter format:

Introduction of the Intervention Strategy

A brief overview of the background and research behind the strategy.

Common Core State Standard

The standard that is associated with this strategy.

What the Intervention Looks Like

Some of the important aspects of the strategy, as well as concepts for developing effective learning.

How the Intervention Works

This step-by-step process shows how to implement the strategy in the classroom. This section is meant to be a guide and should be adjusted as needed to best support students.

ELL Scaffolding

English Language Learners and other students who are socioeconomically or developmentally disadvantaged will benefit from these helpful tips that support fundamental language needs.

Why the Intervention Works

This section covers reasons why many students struggle with academic concepts and skills and why the strategy makes a difference.

Progress Monitoring

The strategy concludes with some brief pointers on how to check for understanding and monitor student progress. Effective progress monitoring requires gathering repeated measures of student performance. There are three primary purposes of progress monitoring in the classroom (National Center on Response to Intervention, 2011):

- Identify students who are struggling to make progress.
- Estimate the rate of student improvement.
- Monitor to provide feedback for adjusting instruction for individual students.

As we observe student progress, it is beneficial to work with students on specific skills in small groups. Through small-group instruction, we can check more thoroughly for how students are learning and how they process information.

As our students grasp these essential intervention strategies, they will become more effective learners at school and beyond.

Special Note: If your 3–6 students struggle to grasp the strategies contained in this book at the Tier I and Tier II levels, then they may need more basic strategies. The authors' book RTI Strategies That Work in the K–2 Classroom *provides additional interventions that will support your students at the most fundamental levels of language and math development.*

Summing It Up

Many of our students need intervention strategies that work. Students in third through sixth grade need to negotiate several hurdles that can affect their future as successful learners. Our students must transition from reading primarily narrative texts focused on stories to reading informational texts that are focused on content knowledge. Our students need to transition from "learning to read" to "reading to learn." A growing number of districts and even entire states have adopted an RTI approach to education. These districts and states have made RTI a priority in addressing struggling students who fall behind their grade-level peers. The demands of school grow with every grade level, and students who have language cracks or develop literacy gaps in the upper elementary grades will soon find that they have unstable knowledge structures that crumble when they need them most. We need to provide high-quality intervention strategies for our students so that they have the tools to negotiate the increasing demands of school and become independent learners. While the strategies in this book will benefit all students, struggling students will enjoy significant benefits from targeted small-group strategies that provide them with more time and more attention from teachers. By providing students with intervention strategies that have high levels of access, engagement, structure, and meaning, we will equip them with the skills to succeed in our classrooms and in their futures. Our students need RTI strategies that work in the core content skills of listening, reading, numeracy, speaking, and writing. We can meet the needs of all our students, as we provide daily small-group interventions that target the specific language, literacy, and learning challenges for each child. Effective classroom intervention strategies provide students with the essential support they need to be academically successful in school. Providing interventions that increase our students' access, engagement, structure, and meaning will enhance their ability to learn. When our students learn to build language relationships, negotiate literacy interactions, and organize their learning, they will be well equipped to succeed in school and will truly become lifelong learners.

Reflection

1. What classroom intervention strategies do you use on a regular basis to improve reading, listening, numeracy, speaking, and writing for students who need RTI support?

2. What intervention strategies would you like to add to your instructional toolbox or classroom-intervention quiver?

2

Grades 3–6 Listening Intervention Strategies

*"To listen well is as powerful a means
of influence as to talk well,
and is as essential to all
true conversation."*

—Chinese Proverb

Kenny glances around the classroom and all the little things swirl around his head. The ticking clock, the scratch of pencils; Marquez is poking Rachel in the back of her head. The air conditioning unit in his classroom coughs before slowing down and turning off. His fourth-grade teacher, Ms. Penny, is talking in the front of the room, yet none of what she says makes sense. His teacher's words seem to be drowned out by a sea of other interests, and he thinks about yesterday's games on the ball field. The objective of the day's lesson completely escapes him. His mind wanders around reviewing last night's video games and TV shows. When it is time to do the assignment, Kenny has no idea where to start or why he is doing it. After staring at his desk for a while, Ms. Penny asks Kenny if he needs help. He doesn't respond. She leans down and repeats herself, but Kenny just shrugs his shoulders a bit, still staring at the desk. Ms. Penny gives up and looks for another student to help. It appears another assignment will go unfinished. It's no wonder: Kenny is a distracted learner.

Interventions That Accelerate and Access Learning

The purpose of classroom intervention strategies is to accelerate progress for those students who lack the skills essential to comprehension and learning. The key to successful interventions is a laser-like focus on instruction. Teachers continually ask what they can do to provide intervention strategies that work with their students in the classroom. A growing number of schools and districts have adopted an RTI model of intervention. These schools have made RTI a priority in addressing students who fall behind their grade-level peers. The RTI model provides a framework for outlining who is responsible in schools for initial instructional support for students who struggle to keep up with grade-level standards. You, the classroom teacher, are the key to making RTI work. Yet, the traditional RTI model does little to nothing to outline *how* teachers and the other support staff are to use research-based intervention strategies to target the specific needs of students.

Many questions arise as teachers and administrators consider the diverse situations our students face. We know that frequent and repeated opportunities to engage in learning strategies will benefit kids, but there is a lot to cover. The issues our students bring to the table are extensive. The interventions need to start early in school. Many students, particularly ELLs, the socio-economically disadvantaged, and struggling readers need support in accessing the fundamental language skills (e.g., academic language) and literacy processes (e.g., interactive input and output) that lead to successful learning. Waiting for issues to resolve themselves without targeted help only puts our students on a treadmill of repeated difficulty. Intervention strategies should be provided as soon as learning problems begin to manifest. When schools consider adopting an RTI model, the emphasis focuses on placing students in regular classrooms rather than sending them off to portables or classrooms that specialize in struggling students (e.g., Title I, ELL, Special Ed). This is a very positive opportunity, but only if the regular classroom teacher also receives additional strategies to effectively meet the additional instructional needs of these struggling students. Ultimately, good intervention strategies come from good instruction and provide all students access to learning.

Instructional Repertoire

When searching for strategies that will help children master their learning objectives and core standards, it is important that we provide multiple methods for students to access the learning. We need to start with building our own personal capacity before we can really begin to build the professional capacity of the organization. The gap in achievement persists even though greater attention from management is directed to it each day. As we have noted, way too many of the students in our schools need intervention. This intervention does not require increasing the amount of dollars spent or the size of the central office. It requires teachers to increase the number of instructional arrows they have in their intervention quiver. In their study of instructional practice, Hoy & Miskell (2002) found that teachers typically use only a handful of strategies. "Moreover, ecological research in classrooms repeatedly finds that teachers rely on just three or four instructional routines to accomplish the majority of their instructional work" (p. 134).

It is helpful for us as classroom teachers to ask ourselves, "What are the barriers that might get in the way for our students?" The barriers might be, for example, the language the adults use to explain a task or the amount of work a child is asked to do without help. Some may have processing issues, like visual tracking. Others may have attention issues, such as Attention Deficit Hyperactive Disorder (ADHD) or Attention Deficit Disorder (ADD). Still others may be so emotionally overwhelmed by their family circumstances that "doing school" requires extra support and attention to their day-to-day ability to participate. In planning, teachers might consider overcoming these barriers by, for example, pre-teaching concepts or key vocabulary, using the child's home language, or incorporating mixed-ability collaborative small-group work or alternative methods of re-teaching concepts. They might support learning by using in a targeted way concrete materials, buddying, and any additional available adult support.

We should ask ourselves several questions in regards to improving our students' access and success.

Do I make sure that

♦ all the children can see and hear me and any resources I am using by making sure that background noise is avoided where possible, the light source is in front of me not behind, and the children's seating is carefully planned?

♦ I check for understanding of instructions by, for example, asking pupils to explain them in their own words?

- tasks relate to work already addressed in whole-class teaching or shared reading or writing so that the child has an example to follow?

- new or difficult vocabulary is clarified, written up, displayed, and consistently checked to verify students have access to the language, literacy, and learning they need?

- I use buddying for seating and paired or partner work by, for example, pairing a more settled child with a child who finds concentration difficult or a more able child with a less able one?

- I give time or support before responses are required by allowing, for example, personal thinking time or partner talk or by persisting with progressively more scaffolding until the child can answer correctly?

- where extra adult support is available, I plan for pupils who need it to be pre-prepared or pre-tutored when this would help them to access the lesson?

- tasks are clearly explained or modeled—there are checks for understanding, task cards or concept posters that provide reminders, and clearly explanations of time available and expected outcomes?

- students arc provided with and regularly reminded of resources, such as relevant material from a whole-class session kept on display, word lists or mats, dictionaries of terms, glossaries, number lines, and tables squares, to help them be independent?

- I have made arrangements, such as buddying, adult support, taping, or bilingual dictionaries, where necessary to ensure that children can access written text or instructions?

Our students gain a lot when we provide a broader repertoire of instructional and intervention strategies. Morrow et al. (2007) note that students "develop a sense of security" when a variety of engaging intervention strategies are consistently provided in the classroom. They begin to feel that the teacher will help them succeed, even if they don't understand the material when it is first explained. The use of additional strategies enables students to see a concept from different angles, reinforcing what they already understand and solidifying their comprehension. The rest of this chapter includes five intervention strategies that will help your students master the Common Core State Standards and develop their listening skills in all areas of learning.

Listening Intervention #1:
Root Words

Students need to attune themselves to listening to how words play together to create meaning. Helping students become more aware of the relationships between words is important in developing their abilities to listen, read, speak, and write effectively. Yet, of all the basic communication skills, we often give listening short shrift and the least amount of attention. Kasper & Babbitt (2000) note that "there are few that address listening and speaking skills. This is unfortunate because academic success requires competence not only in reading and writing, but also in listening and speaking" (p. 227).

One way students can become great comprehenders is by learning to identify root words. Many of the words in the English language come from other languages such as Greek or Latin. Helping students become aware of this insight will help them learn new words effectively as they analyze and understand the meaning behind the root components of many of the words in the English language. According to Trisha Callela (*Greek and Latin Roots, Grades 4–8*),

> Beginning at grade three the national standards require that students use their knowledge of prefixes and suffixes to determine the meaning of words, and that they use their knowledge of root words to determine the meaning of unknown words within a passage. (p. 3)

As we introduce each intervention strategy throughout the book, we will provide the Common Core State Standards that highlight the need for our students to develop competency and even mastery of these particular concepts and skills. Consider the following sixth-grade language standards for root words:

Common Core State Standards

Grade 3: Determine or clarify the meaning of unknown and multiple-meaning word and phrases based on grade 3 reading and content, choosing flexibly from a range of strategies.

♦ Use a known root word as a clue to the meaning of an unknown word with the same root (e.g., *company, companion*).

Continued

> Grade 6: Determine or clarify the meaning of unknown and multiple-meaning words and phrases based on grade 6 reading and content, choosing flexibly from a range of strategies.
>
> ◆ Use common, grade-appropriate Greek or Latin affixes and roots as clues to the meaning of a word (e.g., *audience, auditory, audible*).

What the Root Words Intervention Looks Like

Knowing roots can help students understand the meaning of new words. A root is a fundamental part of a word. Like tree roots give a tree a foundation, root words help a word stand up and give the word its basic meaning. This strategy will help students become much more aware of words and how they are constructed beyond the letter and syllable standpoint. In addition, students will get better at word analysis. This is an important skill for students to develop because it allows them to add new words to their vocabulary more easily (Scanlon, Anderson, Sweeney, 2010). Word analysis considers three components of a word: the prefix, the root, and the suffix. The prefix is the part of the word that comes at the beginning, and the suffix comes at the end of the word and completes it. The root provides the word's core meaning. More than 60 percent of the English language is made up of root definitions that come from Greek or Latin. Furthermore, the English language also has cognates that are similar to 30 percent of Spanish words (Colorín Colorado). This is the case because so many English and Spanish words find their origin in Greek and Latin roots. Studying words through root meanings can unlock vocabulary for students throughout their lives. When prefixes or suffixes are added to root words they make up the full meaning of a word.

$$\text{Prefix} \quad \rightarrow \quad \text{Root} \quad \rightarrow \quad \text{Suffix}$$

Figures 2.1, 2.2, and 2.3 show some common roots, prefixes, and suffixes.

Figure 2.1 Common Roots

Root	Meaning	Examples
ab, abs	away	abnormal
a, ad	move towards	accept, advance
aero	air	aeronautics, aerosol

Root	Meaning	Examples
agri, agro	field	agriculture
ambi	both	ambidextrous
ami	friend	amicable
an	not, without	an
anti	move towards	antidote
ante	before, prior to	antecedent
aqu	water	aquarium
archa	ancient	archaic
arct	cold, north pole	arctic
arist	excellence	aristocrat
astro	star	astrology
aud	hearing, sound	audible, auditory
auto	self-directed	automatic
ben	good	beneficial
bibl	book	bibliography, bible
bio	life	biology, biosphere
brev	brief, short time	brevity
jud	judge	judicial, prejudice
camp	field	encampment, campground
can	sing	incantation
cand	glowing	incandescent, candelabra
cap	head	captain, capital
carbo	coal	carbohydrate, carbon
cav	hollow	cavity, concave
ced, cess	go	process, recede
cent	hundred	percent
centr	center	central
chrom	color	chromatic
chron	time	chronological
clar	clear	clarity, clairvoyance
clem	mild	clemency
cogn	know	metacognitive, cognates
contra	against	contrast, contradict

Root	Meaning	Examples
corn	horn	unicorn, cornucopia
corpor	body	corporation, corporal
cosmo	universe	cosmopolitan, cosmos
cracy	government	aristocracy, democracy
cred	believe, trust	incredible, credulity
cruc	cross	crucible
cycl	circular	tricycle
de	away from	detract
dem	people	democracy
dens	thick	density
dent	tooth	dental, indent
dict	say, speak	dictation, diction
doc	teach	indoctrinate, doctoral
dom	home	domesticate, domicile
duc, duct	lead	conduct
dur	hard	durable, endure
dyna	power	dynamic, dynamite, dynasty
err	stray	error, errant
ex	out of	exterior, exclude, extreme
fact	make	factory, manufacture
fend, fens	prevent	defend, offense
flict	strike	inflict, conflict
flu, flux	flow	influx, confluence
form	shape	conform, formation
graph	written	graphic, telegraph
hydr	water	hydrated, dehydrate
logy	study of	biology, psychology
meter	measure	perimeter, thermometer
micro	small	micrometer, microscope
morph	shape	morpheme
nym	name	antonym, synonym
phil	love	philosophy, philanthropist
phobia	fear	claustrophobia, arachnophobia

Root	Meaning	Examples
phon	sound	telephone, symphony
photo/phos	light	photograph, phosphorous
pseudo	false	pseudonym, pseudoscience
psych	self, soul	psychic, psychologist
scope	view	microscope, telescope
techno	skill, art	technology, technique
tele	far away	television, telephone
therm	heat	thermostat, thermal
voc	voice	vocal, advocate
struct	build	structure, construction
spect	to look	inspector, spectator
sent	to send, to feel	consent, resent
sect	to cut	dissection, section
scrib/scrip	to write	inscribe, prescription
rupt	to break	bankrupt, rupture
port	to carry	portal, transport
pater	father	paternal, paternity
mater	mother	maternity, material
multi	many	multiplex, multiply
mort	death	mortified, mortician
ject	to throw	subjection, rejection
fract	to break	fraction, microfracture
fort	strength	fortify, fortress
mater	mother	maternity, material
multi	many	multiplex, multiply
mort	death	mortified, mortician

Figure 2.2 Common Prefixes

Prefix	Meaning	Examples
anti-	against	antibiotic, antigen
bi-	two	bicycle, biannual
de-	opposite	devalue

Prefix	Meaning	Examples
dis-	not, opposite	disappoint
en-, em-	cause to	enact, empower
fore-	before, front	foreshadowing, foreman
in-, im-	inside	income, impulse
inter-	between	interruption
mid-	middle	midfielder, midsection
mis-	wrong	misspell, mischief
non-	not	nonfat, nonsense
over-	too much	overeat
pre-	before	preview
re-	again	redo, rewrite
semi-	half, part	semitrailer, semifinal
tri-	three	tricycle, trident
sub-	under	subway
super-	above, beyond	superman
trans-	across	transmit, transfer
un-	not, opposite	unusual

Figure 2.3 Common Suffixes

Suffix	Meaning	Examples
-able, -ible	is, can do	capable, responsible
-al, -ial	have characteristics of	universal, facial
-ed	verb form, past tense and participles	walked, chatted
-en	made of	golden
-er, -or	person, one who	teacher, professor
-er	more	taller, bigger
-est	most	tallest, biggest
-ful	full of	mindful, helpful
-ic	have characteristics of	poetic, heretic

Suffix	Meaning	Examples
-ing	verb form, past participle	listening, opening
-ion, -tion	action, process	motion, edition, sedition
-ity, -ty	state of	activity, society
-ive	adjective form of noun	active, sensitive, motive
-less	without	helpless, reckless
-ly	state of	lovely, homely
-ment	state of being	contentment
-ness	condition	happiness
-ous	have qualities of	conscious
-s, -es	more than one	trains, bicycles
-y	characterized by	nasty, misty
-ian	individual	musician, mortician

Not all words have a prefix or a suffix, yet words that come from Greek and Latin origins do have a root word that provides the core meaning for the definition of the word.

How the Root Words Intervention Works

1. **Explain to students** that words in the English language come from many different language origins.
2. **Words are often made up of a combination** of smaller root meanings.
3. **Provide instruction on word parts:** prefixes, roots, and suffixes.
4. **Outline to students** the Create-a-Word game directions (see the next page).
5. **Ask students to combine** the prefixes, roots, and suffixes.
6. **Invite each student to develop his or her own Create-a-Word game** with at least 10 different roots.
7. **Students should select** their own combination of prefixes, roots, and suffixes.
8. **When students hear root words in class,** they should be asked to identify the meanings of the Greek and Latin roots.

The following activity provides an example of how to get students to work with roots, prefixes, and suffixes. It will help them see how to combine elements to create words. An example of student work is shown in Figure 2.4.

Create-a-Word Game

Directions: Please select at least one prefix or one suffix to go along with the root word to create a word. Use your dictionaries to confirm the word and its proper spelling.

Prefix	Root	Suffix
in-	cred	-ible
sub-	terr	-ulous
trans-	port	-anean
re-	consider	-ation
un-	complete	-able
de-	believe	-ion
pre-	activate	-tion
inter-	lax	-ing
pro-	act	-ation
	loc	-ive
	ceed	-s, -es
	dic	
	ject	

ELL Scaffolding

Ask students to work in pairs with ELL students as they complete the Create-a-Word game, so that ELLs can ask questions and receive peer support. Or, work with ELL students in small groups to support their understanding.

Why the Root Words Intervention Works

The root words intervention is effective for several different reasons. This strategy works because it is an engaging strategy. Students like the challenge of putting parts of words together into new combinations. In many ways the activity feels like a game that allows them to compete with themselves

Figure 2.4 **Students' Work on the Root Words Intervention**

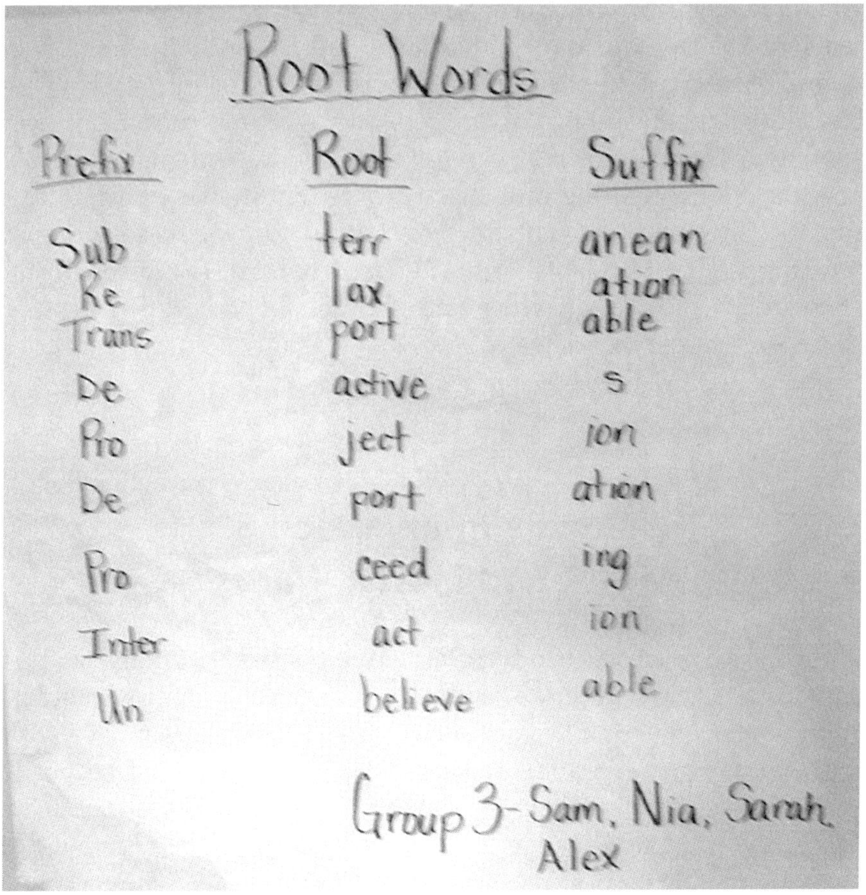

Root Words

Prefix	Root	Suffix
Sub	terr	anean
Re	lax	ation
Trans	port	able
De	active	s
Pro	ject	ion
De	port	ation
Pro	ceed	ing
Inter	act	ion
Un	believe	able

Group 3 - Sam, Nia, Sarah, Alex

and their peers. Students also like devising the Create-a-Word game for their peers to see if they can figure out the combination of root meanings. Students become much more aware of words and how they come to create meaning. Just as it is important for kids to learn that letters and syllables combined can make words, it is important for kids to learn that roots, prefixes, and suffixes are also used to create the words we use in the English language. They learn that words are often a combination of root meanings. Because Spanish and English share many root word origins, mastering root words can benefit ELLs who speak Spanish. Students also benefit by reviewing the origins of root words that are already a part of their vocabulary. As students interact, arrange, and combine the root meanings into larger words, they will learn the meanings of these larger words as well. Students will become aware of word origins and start recognizing additional connections among words.

Progress Monitoring for the Root Words Intervention

This strategy allows you to check students' ability to put words together. Students who struggle may need additional small group instruction to see words in a variety of scenarios. The important part of this strategy is that students develop their word awareness and see how root meanings can be combined. Throughout the school year, provide students opportunities to show the ever increasing number of words that they are adding to their vocabulary. Have students who are strong in word awareness and analysis work with struggling students. Quiz students from time to time on the meaning of the root words to see who needs additional help. Students should be asked to provide the meanings of root words that come up when listening and reading.

Listening Intervention #2: Brick and Mortar Words

Students are faced with an increasing number of vocabulary words they need to learn. Each year students must learn more content vocabulary. In addition to learning content vocabulary (bricks), students must also learn the academic language (mortar) of school. Building a foundation of academic language is crucial to bridging the achievement gap (Scarcella, 2003). Students who are presented academic language across the curriculum are given a mental foundation for building meaningful learning. The types of conversations and breadth of language used in many homes creates a potential divide that places many students at a significant literacy and learning disadvantage before they even enter school. Research by Hart and Risley (2003) revealed that students from low socioeconomic homes come to school with half the vocabulary compared to their kindergarten classmates from high socioeconomic homes. The research showed this language gap appeared as soon as age three, even before students ever come to school. This is why interventions, and specifically language interventions, need to begin in kindergarten. In addition to starting early, these interventions need to continue for several years for low socioeconomic students. The research shows that it takes at least five to seven years for poor students to bridge the language gap that dramatically affects the achievement gap (Barone, Mallet, & Hong Xu, 2005). When we deliver academic instruction that scaffolds academic language, develops concept knowledge, and engages learners in patterns of practice that will keep these learners in school through high school graduation, learning will become easier and seem more "natural" (Lave and Wenger, 1991). Most importantly, academic language provides the foundation and background knowledge for students to more fully engage in activities that require academic rigor. Let's take a quick look at what the Common Core State Standards say on this matter.

Common Core State Standards

Grade 4: **Acquire and use accurately grade-appropriate general academic and domain-specific words and phrases**, including those that signal precise actions, emotions, or states of being (e.g., *quizzed, whined, stammered*) and that are basic to a particular topic (e.g., *wildlife, conservation,* and *endangered* when discussing animal preservation).

Grade 5: **Determine the meaning of general academic and domain-specific words and phrases** in a text relevant to a grade 5 topic or subject area.

What the Brick and Mortar Words Intervention Looks Like

Explaining academic language and providing effective interventions in academic language may be the single most important thing we do for our struggling students. Academic language allows students to develop academic concepts and identify academic patterns that can dramatically boost the coherency of the curriculum and content of school. Smiley and Salsberry (2007) note that "academic language proficiency must be systematically developed and explicitly taught across all language areas" (p. 23). Even though academic language is such a vital part of schooling, it often is overlooked because some students develop it naturally at home; however, others never do obtain it. As a result, 25 percent of our nation is functionally illiterate (Johnson, 2009) and we have a 29 percent dropout rate (Alliance for Education, 2009). So, let's take another look at the fundamental aspects of comprehension graphically outlined in Figure 2.5 (page 40), the Reading/ Language Arts Framework (California State Curriculum Framework, 2008). Note how academic language is vital for developing listening and reading comprehension.

As stated, there are two parts of academic language: brick and mortar. If all students are to be successful in school, it is important for each of them to learn both the brick and the mortar words of school. First let's look at the bricks. The bricks are the general academic language that makes up important content vocabulary:

Figure 2.5 Creating a Framework for Reading

DECODING Learning to Read					COMPREHENSION Reading to Learn				
Word Recognition Strategies				Fluency	Academic Language			Comprehension Strategies	
Concepts of Print	Phonemic Awareness	Phonics	Sight Words	Automaticity	Background Knowledge	Brick and Mortar Vocabulary	Syntax and Text Structure	Comprehension Monitoring	(Re)organizing Text

Adapted from John Shefelbine/Developmental Studies Center

Academic Language Bricks

♦ **Science Bricks**: photosynthesis, atom, cell, evaporation, energy, radiation temperature, velocity

♦ **Mathematics Bricks**: fraction, division, exponent, subtraction, pie chart, equation, congruent, angle

♦ **Social Studies Bricks**: democracy, culture, bureaucracy, capitalism, civil rights, economy, immigration

♦ **Language Arts Bricks**: plot, literary devices, prepositional phrase, theme, predicate, character, punctuation

The mortar words comprise the specific academic language that binds, ties, and glues together the meaning of all content areas learned at school. Learning the academic mortar words is critical for students to be successful in every aspect of school. Just as mortar is formed out of sand, water, and cement, academic language mortar also has three parts:

Academic Language Mortar

♦ **Action Mortar Words:** Words that show up on state standards, classroom activities, and academic assessments.

♦ **Transition Mortar Words:** Words that transition between sentences and paragraphs.

- **Concept Mortar Words:** Words that explain general concepts that are used in a variety of content areas.

Consider the following examples of academic language mortar words outlined by the various grade levels. (Selected examples are from *Academic Language! Academic Literacy!* Complete lists can be found in Appendix A on page 181 and in Johnson 2009 by Corwin Press.)

Examples of Third-Grade Academic Language Mortar Words

- **Action Words:** achieve, assess, believe, clarify, demonstrate, settle, transport

- **Transition Words:** as, frequently, eventually, immediately, instead, until, while

- **Concept Words:** academic, attitude, balance, concept, data, objective, quality

Examples of Fourth-Grade Academic Language Mortar Words

- **Action Words:** anticipate, conserve, devote, nurture, translate, supervise

- **Transition Words:** additionally, for example, importantly, similarly

- **Concept Words:** authority, character, equality, principles, structure, technology

Examples of Fifth-Grade Academic Language Mortar Words

- **Action Words:** approach, commit, enable, involve, navigate, regulate, synthesize

- **Transition Words:** besides, even though, furthermore, on the other hand

- **Concept Words:** challenge, feature, opinion, sample, scope, series, technical

Examples of Sixth-Grade Academic Language Mortar Words

- **Action Words:** accumulate, dedicate, differentiate, integrate, notify, restore

- **Transition Words:** contrastingly, even when, perhaps, therefore, simultaneously

- **Concept Words:** abstract, component, habit, logic, scheme, values, viewpoint

While it seems obvious to us that our students need to master the content vocabulary (brick) of school, it is much less apparent how vital the academic language (mortar) is to providing a proper foundation and the means for binding together these content bricks of learning. So, now that we have a greater appreciation for the importance of this strategy, let's look at some ways to make sure our kids get it.

How the Brick and Mortar Words Intervention Works

1. **Provide instruction and make sure that students understand both parts of academic language** and know the four types of brick words and the three types of mortar words.

2. **Show students the academic language word lists for their grade level** and encourage them to master these words throughout the school year.

3. **Place students in pairs and ask them to pick a passage** or paragraphs from a textbook, and have them do word analysis or identify key terminology for that selection.

4. **Invite students to listen to their partner read from a textbook** as they first identify various brick words and mortar words and then write them down.

5. **Ask the partner who reads** to add additional brick words and mortar words to the list.

6. **After students have written down various brick and mortar words,** they should identify the brick categories (e.g., math, social studies) and the mortar categories (e.g., actions, transitions, and concepts).

7. **Bring students back to a whole-group discussion** of the importance of the brick words and the mortar words and how they contribute to understanding and meaning.

8. **Invite students to continue to recognize** key academic vocabulary brick words and academic language mortar words as they listen in class.

Special note: The next intervention in this chapter as well as others also provide a strategy for learning the academic vocabulary and language of brick and mortar in more detail for those words that are key contributors to understanding meaning.

Why the Brick and Mortar Words Intervention Works

This intervention works because students need academic language to hold their learning together cohesively. Students from low socioeconomic backgrounds and English Language Learners particularly benefit from explicit instruction and support in learning academic language. Understanding the action, transition, and complex concept words of academic language will help students access difficult textbooks, achieve on state assessments, and become better writers. As students become familiar with all of the foundational words for their grade level, they will be able to read and write more effectively. During each activity students will become better at recognizing the brick of specific content language and mortar of general academic language. Students who are word conscious and develop greater awareness of important academic vocabulary and academic language will increase the size of their overall vocabulary.

Progress Monitoring for the Brick and Mortar Words Intervention

Becoming attuned to how many academic language terms students use and how frequently they use them in the classroom is an important skill for teachers to develop. In turn the teacher wants to help students become attuned to recognizing and using academic language in the discussions and activities of the classroom. Students should be taught explicitly two to three general academic language (mortar) words, in addition to any new content-specific-language (brick) words each week. Teachers should quiz students frequently on the academic language words for their grade level and on the words in the previous grade-level lists that they should master. Students who struggle with certain words should work with the teacher in small-group instruction to practice the academic language words. The students should be provided examples from the textbook, from test-release items, and other sources that use the words in academic contexts. The most important words for students to know are the action, transition, and concept words that cut across all content areas of school. Students can also be given bonus points for including targeted academic language words in their writing, since academic language is also the formal language of effective writing.

Listening Intervention #3:
Academic Language Graphic Organizer

Acquiring new vocabulary is a critical component of learning. There is a strong correlation between the size of a student's working vocabulary and the rate at which the student learns (Nation, 2001). Students need a systematic method for learning new vocabulary that will increase their learning capacity. Many methods that teachers traditionally use to add vocabulary for their students are ineffective. Practices like looking up words in the dictionary and copying down the definitions may in fact reduce students' desire to learn new vocabulary. Some students specifically mention that copying definitions out of the dictionary and writing down made-up sentences are great examples of busywork at school. Increasing vocabulary for ELLs and struggling readers is a vital part of developing effective learners. The Academic Language Graphic Organizer provides a thorough and engaging process for helping students learn new vocabulary so that they truly remember the new words and can use them effectively in learning activities.

What the Academic Language Graphic Organizer Intervention Looks Like

The Academic Language Graphic Organizer is specifically designed to expand your students' awareness of words and increase their depth of understanding these words. The graphic organizer uses contrast, comparison, pictures, examples, symbols, non-examples, and working definitions tailored to each student's understanding. Expert learners of vocabulary think of new words in terms of comparing and contrasting the word to other words they know, visualizing pictures that symbolically represent the word, developing a working definition, and thinking of examples and non-examples. Many students, especially ELLs, struggle with grade-level vocabulary.

Academic language provides the means to understand and effectively communicate the actions, transitions, and relationships among the types of knowledge that are valued at school.

Seven Aspects of the Academic Language Graphic Organizer (Figure 2.6)

1. The word is written by the student in the middle of the graphic organizer.

2. Students write down several synonyms of the word.

3. Students list several examples of how the word may be used in context.

4. Students write down a working definition that encapsulates the meaning for them in simple terms.

5. Students draw a picture that symbolizes the meaning of the word for them.

Figure 2.6 Academic Language Graphic Organizer

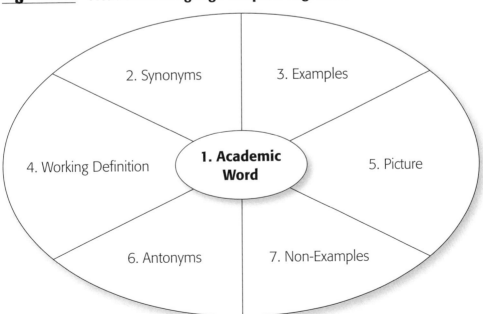

6. Students write down several antonyms of the word.

7. Students list several non-examples of how the word is not used.

Each component of this process is important to developing a robust understanding of new words that are added to one's academic vocabulary. This process does take a little bit of time, yet students will get faster and more proficient the more they engage in this vocabulary building activity. Eventually students will learn to analyze and think about the different aspects of words like examples, working definitions, symbolic pictures, and non-examples without even completing the graphic organizer.

Completing the Academic Language Graphic Organizer takes time, so it is important that only those words that are most valuable to your class go through the complete graphic organizer strategy. The best way to identify the most critical words for your class is a strategy that is called Fist-to-Five. While we won't go into detail about this quick assessment, the gist of it is to ask students to raise their hand and hold up the appropriate number of fingers to demonstrate their understanding and confidence with some of the key vocabulary words that will be used in the daily lesson. Students hold up one finger if they do not know the word and five fingers if they know the word well with multiple meanings. Holding up two or three fingers shows that they are only vaguely familiar with the word. By quickly glancing around the room at the number of fingers your students are holding up, you can see which students need the most help and which words need the most attention. This easy assessment strategy allows you to go quickly through a list of words and identify which words the class in general needs additional help to understand. The Fist-to-Five strategy is a fast way to determine which brick words and which mortar words the class should put through the Academic Language Graphic Organizer. So, now let's look at the hows and wherefores of the strategy.

How the Academic Language Graphic Organizer Intervention Works

1. **Provide students with an academic language word** to develop their understanding.

2. **Have students write the academic language word (1) in the middle** of the graphic organizer.

3. **Model the proper pronunciation of the word,** and then have the students say the word out loud chorally.

4. **Students should then identify and write down synonyms (2) of the word** on the graphic organizer.

5. **Students write down examples (3) and a working definition (4)** of the word on the graphic organizer.

6. **Students should draw a picture (5) of the word** on the graphic organizer.

7. **Students should then provide antonyms (6) and non-examples (7)** on the graphic organizer.

8. **After finishing the graphic organizer, the students should share their answers with the class** to provide a variety of antonyms, examples, working definitions, symbolic pictures, antonyms, and non-examples.

9. **Students can write on their graphic organizers** ideas from their classmates that resonate with them.

10. **Make sure to use the words in the course of your lessons,** and give bonus points or positive recognition for those students who identify key brick and mortar words they hear or read.

11. **Ask students to incorporate** the words they learn in their own writing.

Figure 2.7 shows an example of the Academic Language Graphic Organizer using the science brick word *energy*:

Figure 2.7 Sample Academic Language Graphic Organizer for *Energy*

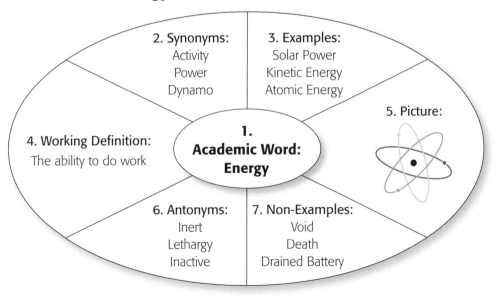

ELL Scaffolding

Ask students to work in pairs with ELL students as they answer questions or fill out graphic organizers, so that ELLs can ask questions and receive peer support.

Why the Academic Language Graphic Organizer Intervention Works

This intervention works because it provides a robust method for helping students learn new academic vocabulary. Again, this ability is so vital to learning that many assessments use vocabulary as a quick and effective way for determining competency. For example, many of you may have taken the Graduate Requisite Exam (GRE) to gain acceptance to graduate school. This university-level assessment devotes two-thirds of its questions to vocabulary definitions and analysis. The thinking goes that if you have a high-level vocabulary then you have high-level concept knowledge, because it is through words that we comprehend and convey our knowledge. If it is important for graduate school, academic language is even more important for students in grades 3–6 if they want to prepare to attend college. So, the Academic Language Graphic Organizer helps students scaffold their learning as they develop their vocabulary comprehension. Students will, over time, begin to visualize a picture and working definition for words because of the organizer. They will also develop their understanding of synonyms and antonyms. This strategy will help them build a robust understanding of language and how language is used to creating meaning.

Progress Monitoring for the Academic Language Graphic Organizer Intervention

Because it is important that students add new words to their working vocabulary, teachers should quiz students to see if they can draw pictures that symbolize words. Eventually, students should be able to fill out the graphic organizer by themselves in a quick fashion. Use the Fist-to-Five strategy to help front-load language for students and assess those specific words with which students need additional support. Knowing what the research says about students' vocabulary development can help teachers anticipate where to target more attention and provide more progress monitoring. Look at the information in Figure 2.8, adapted from Hirsch (2006) and Nagy & Anderson (1984).

Figure 2.8   How a Student's Background Affects Vocabulary Learning

Student's Socioeconomic Background	Estimated Words Learned per Year	Average Words Learned per Day	Average Words Learned per Week
Low	3,000	7	50
Working-class	5,000	12	85
Professional	5,500	14	100

While 90 percent of the words students acquire are learned through inferring, about 10 percent are learned through explicit classroom instruction. So as we monitor progress, we should be very deliberate in the words we choose to explain, track, and make sure students learn. If students struggle with the graphic organizer, work with these students in a small group to monitor their progress as they add new words to their vocabulary until they become proficient at developing a broad understanding.

Listening Intervention #4: Purposeful Prepositions

Gaining a basic understanding of grammar has long been a foundational part of learning the English language. Understanding the role words play in creating meaning can benefit students' ability to learn. Of all the various grammatical parts of speech, prepositions seem to be the most difficult for young students to grasp (Hoffman, 2011). It may be caused by the fact that prepositions are part of prepositional phrases or it may be because prepositions often identify abstract relationships. Consistent observations have shown that prepositions are particularly difficult for English Language Learners (Lems, Miller, & Soros, 2009). Many of our students need help grasping the role prepositions play in comprehending and constructing language. Figure 2.9 (page 50) shows some of the ways to explain the various parts of speech to young students.

Notice that prepositions are "relater" words. They show relationships between two things. The relationship may be a relationship of origin (from), a relationship of time (before), a relationship of space (between), a relationship

Figure 2.9 Explaining the Parts of Speech

Part of Speech	Role Played
Noun	Namer
Pronoun	Renamer
Verb	Shows Action or Links
Adjective	Describer
Adverb	Describer
Conjunction	Joiner
Preposition	Relater
Interjection	Shows Emotion

of orientation (in), a relationship of purpose (for), and so forth. Making these relationships explicit for students helps them understand the role prepositions play in understanding others. Effective students are able to listen to a sentence and pick out the noun, verb, preposition, and other parts of speech. This process typically takes time, and students will need plenty of practice to become proficient.

Common Core State Standards

Grade 5: Demonstrate command of the conventions of standard English grammar and usage when writing or speaking.

♦ Explain the function of conjunctions, **prepositions**, and interjections in general and their function in particular sentences.

Grade 3: Acquire and use accurately grade-appropriate conversational, general academic, and domain-specific words and phrases, including those that signal spatial and temporal relationships (e.g., After dinner that night we went looking for them).

What the Purposeful Prepositions Intervention Looks Like

One of the most difficult concepts to teach explicitly is how to differentiate between various prepositions. English learners will say with confidence, "I am

Figure 2.10 Commonly Used Prepositions

about	above	across	after	against	along
among	around	as	at	before	behind
below	beside	between	by	down	during
except	for	from	in	inside	into
near	next	of	off	on	onto
out	over	past	since	than	through
to	toward	under	until	up	upon
with	without				

in the floor." Correcting the preposition doesn't seem to do the trick until the visual concept of each preposition is conveyed, confirmed, and constructed.

A preposition describes a relationship between other words in the sentence. Figure 2.10 is a list of commonly used prepositions.

Students need to understand that because prepositions show a relationship between two things, every preposition has an object of the preposition. Figure 2.11 shows some examples.

Consider the following prepositions that are grouped in the categories of time, place, and orientation. Let's help students order the prepositions into relevant groupings that will help tag what the purpose of the prepositions is in a sentence. For example, ask the students to identify prepositions related to time.

Figure 2.11 How Prepositional Phrases Work

Examples of Prepositional Phrases	
The dog *by* the **car**	Relationship between dog and car
The kid *from* **Mexico**	Relationship between kid and Mexico
The cat *in* the **hat**	Relationship between cat and hat
A bridge *over* the **river**	Relationship between bridge and river
A gallon *of* **milk**	Relationship between gallon and milk

TIME: after, before, during, past, since, until, upon

Now, let's look at the prepositions that identify placement. These tell us where something is located in relation to another item: above; below, across, after, against, among, around, before, behind, between. Have the students find the rest of the place prepositions!

PLACE: above, across, at, before, behind, inside

The orientation prepositions present the most difficulty for students and require the most repetition with Say it, Show it, Write it. They require that the students infer and guess about the relationships between two objects.

ORIENTATION: except, without, against, as, off, to

In the examples in Figure 2.11 on the previous page, the object of the preposition comes after the preposition, and the object of the preposition creates a relationship between both nouns.

How the Purposeful Prepositions Intervention Works

1. **This strategy requires that you first use a small ball** to show how prepositions create relationships.

2. **Show students the ball and say,** "The ball is *in* my hand." This shows the relationship between the ball and the hand.

3. **Have students repeat** what you say, pretending to put a ball in their hands.

4. **Next say,** "The ball is *under* my hand." And have the students repeat and pretend to do as you have done.

5. **You can ask a student to come up in front of the class and model** what you are saying about the ball in each example. See Figure 2.12.

6. **Have students repeat what is said and modeled for them.** Repeat this until you have gone through the most of the common prepositions (many of them are listed in Figure 2.10 on the previous page).

7. **After students have heard the statement,** repeated it, and modeled it, ask them to draw a picture representing each preposition so that they will remember its meaning.

Figure 2.12 How Prepositions Show Relationships

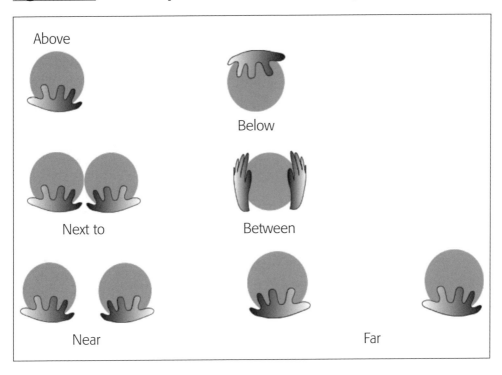

8. **Then have students write a sentence** using the preposition.

9. **Ask them to use information from the classroom** to make the sentences real. For example:
   - She has two red balls next to the chair.
   - I like my red ball in my desk.
   - Steve likes the red ball against the door.

10. **Helping students understand patterns among prepositions** can also help them better identify and use prepositions effectively.

Again, this strategy requires that you first use a small ball. Show the ball to the students and say, "The ball is *in* my hand." Have students repeat what you say, pretending to put (or actually putting) a ball in their hands. "Now, the ball is *under* my hand." Have them repeat what you say and what you show. Do this until you have gone through the most common prepositions. Figure 2.13 on the next page shows a student working with prepositions.

Figure 2.13 Prepositions Intervention

Figure 2.14 Concept Poster for Prepositions

Ask the students to demonstrate what each preposition means using the ball. Have the students watch one another and see where they are placing the ball for the word. See if they share a common understanding. The picture on the right (Figure 2.14) shows a concept poster that can be provided to help students remember many of the common prepositions that show relationship.

Why the Purposeful Prepositions Intervention Works

This strategy works because prepositions can be very difficult for students to learn in the upper elementary grades. Both the adjective prepositional phrases and the adverbial prepositional phrases are often concepts that are lost on kids. Prepositions demonstrate a relationship between a noun and the object of the preposition. Students who can readily recognize prepositions and distinguish them from other parts of the sentence develop greater control as writers. Providing a reference poster that is hung on the wall and can be viewed by students will help students remember and use the prepositions effectively. Prepositions must be understood with automaticity, and the lesson must create concrete tags to the meaning of the prepositions and their usage. Listening is always the initial step—it brings the language alive and makes the learning tangible. Make sure that students can show how the preposition creates relationships. To make a lesson tangible and meaningful, always try to tie something memorable to the language lesson that is foundational—hence, the title of this activity "purposeful prepositions." The preposition tells us *where* to look for things (place): behind, over, under, in, out, up, down; *when* something might have happened (time): during, before, after, next, since, beyond; and *how* close an object is to us: near, next, against, across, toward, behind, below (orientation). These are little words with great purpose!

Progress Monitoring for the Purposeful Prepositions Intervention

One of the most important transitions to manage cognitively is the shift from concrete to abstract, or abstract to concrete. A quick way to check for understanding is to provide a sentence stem and ask students to add a prepositional phrase. Working in a small group, use a red ball, call out the prepositions, and ask students to place the ball in a position describing the words. After the students have heard the statement, repeated it, and demonstrated they understood the meaning of the prepositions using the ball, they should be able to use prepositions effectively in their writing. Provide explicit feedback to students, particularly ELLs, who use prepositions imprecisely. If a student uses a preposition imprecisely, you can ask the student to pick a different preposition or ask other students for another preposition that more precisely demonstrates the desired relationship.

Listening Intervention #5: Figures of Speech

Children enjoy the musical qualities of listening to figures of speech. Figures of speech or literacy devices are a collection of language tools that bring words to life. Different figures of speech can evoke vivid images for students. They can create intriguing sounds. Figurative language can make learning much richer and cause the reader to almost reach out and touch the images created by the words (Baumann & Kameenui, 2004). It can create in the mind contrasting images that help listeners remember what they hear. Expert writers use figures of speech liberally. Figurative language creates pictures in the mind of the listener and conveys meaning faster and more vividly. All in all, figures of speech are ways of using words that tantalize the senses. Figurative language is the opposite of literal language. Literal language means exactly what it says, while figurative language includes much more than what it says on the surface. Figurative language is used in children's storybooks, poems, Shakespeare, and modern pop music.

Common Core State Standards

Grade 5: **Demonstrate understanding of figurative language,** word relationships, and nuances in word meanings.

♦ **Interpret figurative language,** including similes and metaphors, in context.

What the Figures of Speech Intervention Looks Like

This strategy is all about increasing students' awareness of language and its power. Young students in grades 3–6 are often unaware of why they enjoy listening to certain language and why other words may be quite boring. Figures of speech are like the fireworks of language that explode into delightful images for the listener. Arthur Quinn (1993) describes it this way: The "figurings" of speech reveal the apparently limitless plasticity of language itself (p. 112).

Figure 2.15   Figures of Speech Categories

Sound	Visual Imagery	Contrast
Rhyme	Simile	Irony
Onomatopoeia	Metaphor	Oxymoron
Alliteration	Personification	Foreshadowing
Assonance	Imagery	Hyperbole
Repetition	Symbol	

The Figures of Speech Intervention is an advanced intervention. What do we mean by that? Like many of the interventions, it helps students at the basic level become more aware of how to learn more successfully. At the same time, it helps students at an advanced level. As students listen to the musical nature of language and recognize the devices being used, they will enhance their basic understanding and learning. Over time, the intervention can elevate their learning as they internalize the skills and become proficient writers themselves of figures of speech. While there are dozens of types of figures of speech, young students should become aware and learn to aurally recognize at least 15 or so figures of speech. The first part of the strategy includes organizing the figures of speech into categories so that students remember them more easily. Three basic categories for figures of speech are sound, visual imagery, and contrast (Figure 2.15).

For young students, the figures of speech that use sound as a learning device may be easiest to recognize and remember. As students move into fourth, fifth, and sixth grade, they should add the visual imagery and contrasting figures of speech to their language toolbox. Figure 2.16 provides examples of core figures of speech, and Figure 2.17 shows a sample classroom poster with illustrations.

Figure 2.16   Core Figures of Speech

Figure of Speech	Examples
Rhyme	quiet riot, sublime rhyme, Tricky Nicky
Onomatopoeia	buzz, pow, zing, bang, kerplunk, wham, crunch, boing

Continued

Figure 2.16 *Continued*

Figure of Speech	Examples
Alliteration	Susie sold seashells by the seashore. Peter Piper picked a peck of pickled peppers.
Assonance	How now, brown cow. Baa baa, Black Sheep.
Repetition	I'll huff and I'll puff and I'll blow the house down. Run away, little boy, run away.
Simile	She swims like a dolphin. He was as tough as a bulldog. Similes are like candy to a reader.
Metaphor	The whole world is a stage. John is a real pig. Susie dated a snake.
Personification	The tree limbs reached out and grabbed her coat. The stream sang a tune.
Imagery	The moon glistened and shimmered as it reflected off the lake. The rocket surged forward blowing white billowy clouds of smoke as it exploded off the launchpad.
Symbol	The ant in "The Ant and the Grasshopper" symbolizes hard work and preparation.
Irony	The fire station burnt to the ground. The off-duty police officer received a speeding ticket.
Oxymoron	Jumbo shrimp, bittersweet, virtual reality, deafening silence, silent scream
Foreshadowing	The book *Holes* has lots of foreshadowing in it.
Hyperbole	It cost a million bucks. She ate a thousand of them.

How the Figures of Speech Intervention Works

1. **Introduce students to the concept of figures of speech** and introduce each core figure of speech.

2. **Provide examples of each type of figure of speech** for the students in both spoken and written form.

3. **Ask students to identify the figures of speech** from the examples provided.

4. **Explain the three categories of the figures of speech** to help students recognize their common attributes.

5. **When you read stories that have figures of speech in them, make sure students identify** the example and the type of figure of speech.

6. **Ask students to think of as many examples as possible** of different types of figures of speech.

7. **Have students share their examples out loud** while their peers listen and identify the types of figures of speech.

8. **Ask students to write poetry** that includes their figures of speech.

9. **Have students listen** as others read their poetry out loud.

Figure 2.17 **Figures of Speech Classroom Poster**

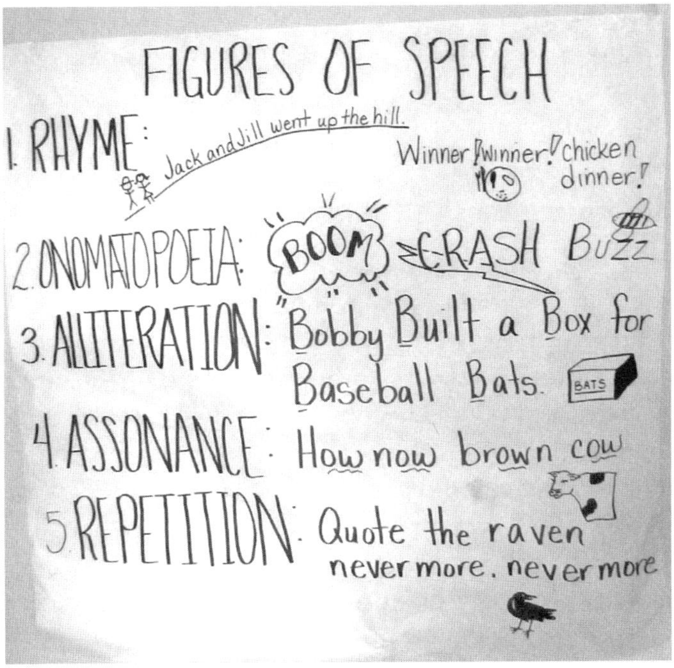

This intervention begins with teaching a handful of the figures of speech in third and fourth grade and then making sure that students have mastered the complete list by the time they enter fifth and sixth grade.

Why the Figures of Speech Intervention Works

This strategy works because students benefit when they become aware of the different devices speakers and authors use to make their writing come to life. Students can organize their understanding by categorizing the different types of figurative language. As students become proficient in this strategy, they will enjoy listening and reading much more. This strategy is like a Cracker Jack box for kids as they will be pleasantly surprised by the figures of speech they identify when listening. They key is for students to become aware of the power of language and how using language effectively can enhance learning. The figures of speech will open up students to the myriad of ways that language can be used. When students eventually learn to incorporate figures of speech into their own writing, they will develop more confidence in their literacy abilities.

Progress Monitoring for the Figures of Speech Intervention

You can check for understanding of the figures of speech intervention by reading examples out loud and then asking students to identify the figure of speech in each example. For individual or small groups, you can use flash cards to check a student's ability to hear figures of speech and recognize the different types. As students become proficient, you will notice that they accurately identify the various figures of speech when they hear them or see them in print. The most complete way for monitoring student progress may be simply by looking at students' use of figurative language in their poetic and formal writing. Having students write simple stanzas of poetry using various figures of speech is a great way for students to gain confidence and showcase their progress.

Summing It Up

We can provide interventions that make a difference for our students. Many of our students struggle to access learning because they lack the language foundation, literacy framework, or academic finishing work. As our students learn the Common Core State Standards, they will progress at grade level. Students who struggle to master the Common Core listening skills through first instruction need targeted interventions. Listening is an underappreciated linguistic skill. Root words, along with prefixes and suffixes, help students understand how words are constructed. Listening to and identifying figurative language will help students expand their appreciation for the role language plays in learning. Many students struggle with identifying prepositions and learning how they are used to provide more description in writing. As students master the academic language for their grade level as well as all of the words in the previous grade-level lists, they will build greater confidence in their abilities to master grade-level standards, to access content-area textbooks, and to succeed on annual state assessments. As students use the graphic organizers to develop routines for learning new academic vocabulary (bricks) and academic language (mortar), they will strengthen their ability to learn words without the use of this scaffold. Academic language graphic organizers help students to develop more robust understandings of the new words they add to their vocabulary. As our students learn to listen to the various aspects of words, they will lay a foundation for becoming better learners.

Reflection

1. How effectively do your students infer, and how many types of inferences are they able to identify?

2. Do your students know the bricks—the general content language—in the four core areas of math, science, language arts, and social studies for their grade level? Do they know the 75 mortar words—the specific academic language for their grade level?

3

Grades 3–6 Reading Intervention Strategies

*"A capacity and taste for reading
gives access to whatever
has already been
discovered by others."*

—Abraham Lincoln

Chandra loved storytime. She enjoyed being all snuggled up on the rug while her teacher read to the class. It was exciting to see the pictures and imagine what's happening in the stories. Of course, that was in kindergarten. Now that Chandra is in fifth grade, things have changed. While they do read in class, the rug is gone and the books have only a few pictures. Now she is asked to read long passages from social studies and science textbooks. While she liked being read to, Chandra dislikes having to read on her own. She avoids reading as much as possible. When asked to read aloud, she just goes through the motions. In fact, it she not only avoids reading, she downright dreads it. At times she even refuses to read out loud in class. Her confidence as a reader and a learner is slipping away. Chandra has become a resistant reader.

The Structure of Language, Literacy, and Learning

There are many things at school that can distract students from interventions. A typical RTI approach lacks high-quality instructional interventions. Educators like the RTI approach and believe that they can make a difference for many students before it becomes too late, yet they know that they need targeted strategies that will make a difference. Because higher percentages of students of color live in poverty, a higher percentage of them have been placed in resource classes. The discrepancy model noted that once a student fell behind several grade levels, many districts would quickly place the student in special education. This model lacks the specific instructional approaches our students need to make the framework really work. Classroom interventions should be provided as early as kindergarten and as soon as it is evident that students lack fundamental reading skills like alphabetic knowledge, phonemic awareness, and phonics. As students advance to grades 3–6, they need support in text comprehension and cognitive reading strategies. It is also important to have the necessary structure in place that can address the learning needs. Webster & Fisher (2001) note that

> Teachers and the instructional approaches they use are funda-
> mental in building students' understanding. Primary among their
> many duties and responsibilities, teachers structure and guide the
> pace of individual, small-group and whole-class work to present
> new material, engage students in learning tasks, and help deepen
> students' grasp of the content and concepts being studied. (p. 2)

As we proceed through the upcoming pages, we will discover the vital role that reading strategies play in student success. These strategies should be provided to students in whole-class scenarios and small-groups in Tier I and Tier II. If students continue to struggle with reading at grade level, they should be provided one-on-one support in reading that provides Tier III interventions. The research on reading reveals that many students begin their educational careers with significant learning disadvantages. These disadvantages often appear even before students start school. For example, many students from poverty come to school with about half of the academic vocabulary of their more privileged peers (Hart & Risley, 2003). Students from poverty, struggling readers, and students with special needs face substantial challenges when they are asked to acquire the language and literacy skills needed for reading success.

Struggling Readers

Identifying the struggling readers in class is important. Students who struggle with reading grade-level texts have difficulty in most every content area. Valencia and Buly (2004) offer six patterns for identifying struggling readers:

1. **Automatic Word Callers** decode text quickly and accurately, but do not read for meaning.
2. **Slow Comprehenders** decode accurately and comprehend well, but process text slowly.
3. **Struggling Word Callers** have difficulty with both word identification and meaning.
4. **Word Stumblers** have trouble with word identification, but they are strong comprehenders of meaning.
5. **Slow Word Callers** decode effectively, yet they read slowly and without meaning.
6. **Disabled Readers** have difficulty with fluency, word identification, and meaning.

Whichever way we define our struggling readers in grades 3–6, it is vital that we provide a variety of interventions that will improve their ability to read. Guiding students' reading, identify key text patterns, and developing inferring skills will help students become better readers. So, let's get into the reading interventions.

Reading Intervention #1: Guided Reading

Our students who become avid readers become better learners. Reading is the primary method by which we access new information. The older we get, the more we must rely on reading to add to our informational understanding. The statement "Leaders are readers!" is simply true. Improving comprehension of learners is particularly important to learners from low-income families who are already facing a language gap, which often means these students face a knowledge gap as well. Guided reading interventions are effective as they provide students opportunities to focus on comprehension while they enjoy the support of their grade-level peers. Guided reading also enhances the development of fluency (Irvin, Meltzer, & Dukes, 2007). Reading fluency, or rate, expression, and automaticity allow readers to concentrate on comprehension. Guided reading also provides a support for increasing students' knowledge of the academic language and content knowledge that is contained in formal reading. Research shows time and time again that students' amount of reading contributes significantly to their ability to learn and retain new knowledge (Pearson & Kamil, 2007).

What the Guided Reading Intervention Looks Like

Guided reading provides opportunities for students to read and work in small groups as they develop greater comprehension. Placing students in small groups of four to five students will give them time to practice reading, listen to others, and reflect on their own understanding of the material being read. Fountas & Pinnell (1996) emphasize the considerable benefits derived from placing students in guided reading groups. The strategies that are emphasized in this chapter can and should be emphasized during guided reading sessions. Biancarosa & Snow (2003) promote the following benefits of engaging in pre-reading, reading, and post-reading sessions during guided reading:

1. **Pre-reading:** preview important vocabulary, make predictions, identify text features

2. **Reading:** notice graphic representations of concepts, ask questions, monitor comprehension of unfamiliar words

3. **Post-reading:** rephrase, summarize, compare ideas with others, determine main points from details

Guided reading helps students become proficient and effective readers. Making reading strategies explicit will draw greater attention to the skills that develop reading comprehension. The time spent reading in small groups will enhance everyone's comprehension.

How the Guided Reading Intervention Works

1. **Allocate 15–20 minutes of time** for each guided reading session.

2. **Divide students into groups of four to five students** according to their reading levels.

3. **Establish a purpose for the reading by identifying through a pre-reading activity,** a cognitive strategy, vocabulary development, or content comprehension that should be analyzed and discussed. (See the cognitive strategies in Figure 3.1.)

4. **The pre-reading time can emphasize many of the other strategies in this chapter,** like predicting, inferring, highlighting key vocabulary, or providing background knowledge.

5. **Students take turns reading and pausing every so often to "think aloud"** and discuss their reading while expressing the comprehension they are developing.

6. **The teacher circulates around the room listening to the readers,** quietly coaching and guiding them by prompting the groups to identify reading strategies that will assist in developing their individual and collective comprehension.

Figure 3.1   Cognitive Reading Strategies

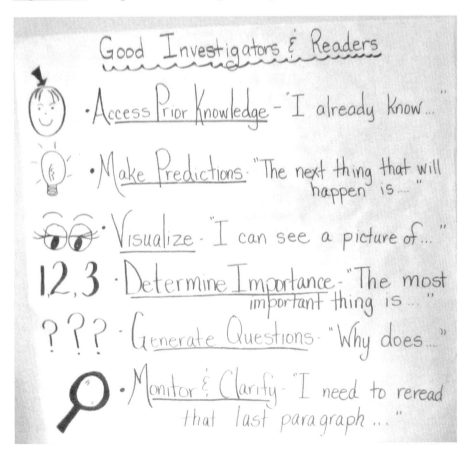

7. **Post-reading time provides the teacher with time to review the lessons learned** and the student's understanding about the content and, more importantly, the reading strategies.

8. **Initially, teachers may want to work with only one group at a time** until they have confidence that the readers in each group understand the purpose and the process for guided reading.

9. **More advanced readers can typically interact effectively on their own** in guided reading groups with only occasional suggestions.

10. **Remind students that the purpose of guided reading is to develop their reading strategies** as well as to add to their content knowledge.

ELL Scaffolding

English Language Learners will often need basic-level texts that have lots of pictures for guided reading. Emphasis on academic vocabulary should be a highlight of every guided reading session. Non-ELL readers should participate in the guided reading so that ELL students can learn from them.

Additional Tips When Implementing Guided Reading Groups

♦ Initially, select easier, more interesting texts for students to read so they can gain confidence in their group.

♦ To keep things fresh, switch up groupings according to ability, interest, or social peers.

♦ Ask students to read at home and report back to their guided reading groups.

♦ Invite parents or community members to assist during guided-reading time so more coaching is available.

♦ Emphasize to students the value of supportive group interactions as much as the importance of effective reading strategies.

♦ Provide time for groups to briefly report their progress to the entire class, and then applaud their efforts.

Why the Guided Reading Intervention Works

This strategy works because students typically enjoy working in small groups. It gives students time to practice their reading out loud in front of others, and at the same time offers them an opportunity to reflect and listen to others. Guided reading supports frequent reading and monitoring comprehension, and it draws attention to the variety of strategies that enhance effective reading skills. Asking students to share their "thinking aloud" with their classmates allows them to receive input and feedback. Students can use Post-it Notes to record their think-aloud thoughts as they read and write down their reflections, which can serve as a running commentary. This running commentary can be helpful when students are asked later to produce an essay or another piece of writing from their reading. Guided reading also allows students to model the teacher's efforts and coach their peers on effective reading strategies. Through guided reading, the strategies of effective readers are explicitly brought out in an authentic reading setting.

Progress Monitoring for the Guided Reading Intervention

The format for leading a guided reading session provides ample opportunity for the teacher to monitor students' progress. It also gives students the time to monitor their own reading strategies, as well as the strategies of their peers. Listen intently as you circulate the classroom, and provide gentle coaching and support. Take the time to identify explicitly the progress that students are making and praise them for their efforts. Make sure that students recognize the insights they are having in their own comprehension. Good readers metacognitively reflect on the information they read, so make sure students reflect on both the content of their reading and the strategies they use to develop comprehension. Guided reading provides the teacher time to monitor students' reading progress and give consistent feedback.

Reading Intervention #2:
Comparing Text Structures

Students' favorite time of day may be story time on the rug with the teacher. While rug-time reading with the teacher typically is reduced as students get older, they still love being read to. The narrative stories that students listen to strengthen their love of reading and learning. During grades 3–6, students need to make several important transitions that will affect their reading habits. One important transition that students need to make is the transition from reading narrative texts to reading more informational texts. This transition is assisted by our students' understanding of various text types and text structures.

What the Comparing Text Structures Intervention Looks Like

Good authors typically organize their writing through consistent text structures that help readers recognize and understand the message being delivered. Knowing the common sets of text structures will help students organize and remember what they read. While all of the narrative text structures follow the same general pattern—background/setting, quest/conflict, action, climax, and resolution—the various types of narrative structures are typically divided into five genres (Figure 3.2). These genres are general categories of writing in which authors have followed consistent patterns. As students are able to identify various narrative genres, they will gain a greater appreciation of reading, and they will be able to remember the story more effectively.

Figure 3.2 Five Narrative Text Genres

Fantasy	Folktale	Historical Fiction	Realistic Fiction	Science Fiction
This type of narrative is make-believe. Stories are set in places that do not exist and are about people and creatures that could not exist, or events that can only happen in our imagination.	This type of narrative includes traditional stories, myths, legends, nursery rhymes, and songs from the past.	This type of narrative is set in the past and could have happened. Stories reconstruct events of past ages and things that could have or did occur.	This type of narrative covers "What if" stories or illusions of reality. Events take place in a contemporary setting and could happen in the real world; characters seem real.	This type of narrative is based on extending physical laws and scientific principles to their logical outcomes. Stories are about what might occur in the future.

Figure 3.3 Four Types of Informational Text Structures

Compare/ Contrast	Descriptive	Cause/Effect	Sequential/ Time-Order
This text structure shows comparisons between similarities of information or a contrast between differences.	This text structure provides detailed description of an event or situation.	This text structure is also called problem/solution. It shows causes for events and then the effects that occur.	This text structure places things in a sequence or in time order.

In addition to learning narrative text genres, students in grades 3–6 need to become familiar with informational text structures. It seems so many textbooks do very little to explicitly point out the common text structures that are regularly used by authors. Dickson, Simmons, and Kame'enui (1998) note that "text structure refers to the organizational features that serve as a frame or pattern to guide and help readers identify important information and logical connections between ideas" (p.251). Informational textbooks and other expository texts typically fall into four types of text structures: cause/effect, descriptive, compare/contrast, and sequential/chronological (Figure 3.3).

Young students take in written words without much analysis. They take most of the written information at face value without much examination. It is critical for all students to be familiar with text structures so that they can better organize their learning in efficient ways that will help them retrieve the information. In addition to understanding the five types of narrative text genres and the four basic types of informational text structures, students benefit when they recognize the differences between these types of texts. Figure 3.4 (Johnson, 2009) provides a great resource for students as they identify the differences between narrative and informative text:

Figure 3.4 Comparing Text Structures and Formats

Narrative Text	Informative Text
Character-oriented towards the actions of a particular character	**Subject-oriented** towards a particular topic or issue
Primary purpose: **to entertain** and to give literary or aesthetic experience	Primary purpose: **to explain**, to present information, or to persuade

Continued

Figure 3.4 *Continued*

Narrative Text	Informative Text
Based on **life experiences** and relationships between or among characters	Based on **abstract concepts** and relationships between or among ideas
Academic language may be less essential with few new words introduced; often contains **dialogue** and many words common in spoken language	**Academic language** is essential to comprehension; introduces many content-specific words and complex sentence structures
Most often employs a **predictable sequenced pattern** along a time line; it conveys a **beginning, middle, and end** of events	Uses a **variety of text patterns**, often in the same text; e.g., compare and contrast, description, cause and effect, and time order or sequence
Links the character's actions or a sequence of events in time order (beginning, middle, and end)	**Links relationships between or among ideas,** from the most important idea to supporting ideas with examples
Has **illustrations** that show actions of characters in colorful detail	Has **charts**, diagrams, facts, pictures, and/or tables
Reader Story **Questions**: Who is the main character? What happened next? How did the problem get solved?	Reader Information **Questions**: What is the main subject? What are the supporting details? How can I use this information?

As students learn to recognize the differences between narrative and informative text structures, they will be able to more easily identify text structures.

How the Comparing Text Structures Intervention Works

1. **Introduce the five parts of narrative text structure** for your students.
2. **Make sure that students can identify these narrative structures** in familiar stories that they know (e.g., "Goldilocks and the Three Bears" and "The Three Little Pigs").
3. **Show students examples of different narrative story genres.** (It may take a week to review narrative text structures and help students identify different story genres.)
4. **Introduce the idea of informational text structures** once students are comfortable with narrative structure and story genres.

5. **Provide examples of the four types of informational text structures** for students. Working with students to create posters of various text structures can serve to remind students of key components of text structures.

6. **Explicitly point out examples of compare/contrast structure** in core texts (e.g., science, social studies).

7. **Explicitly point out examples of descriptive structure** in core texts (e.g., science, social studies).

8. **Explicitly point out examples of cause/effect structure** in core texts (e.g., science, social studies).

9. **Explicitly point out examples of sequential/time order structure** in core texts (e.g., science, social studies).

10. **Ask students to read informational text and highlight** the key compare/contrast, descriptive, cause/effect, or sequential/time-order aspects of the text. (Also see Intervention Strategy #4 in this chapter for more ideas for ensuring students can readily identify text structure.)

ELL Scaffolding

English Language Learners may be the biggest beneficiaries of identifying text structures. ELLs often have limited vocabulary registers. Knowing text structures can help them with comprehension even though they have limited vocabularies. Work with ELLs in small groups so that you can ensure they are identifying various text structures.

Why the Comparing Text Structures Intervention Works

This intervention is extremely effective because it provides a clear context for students to organize the vast amounts of information they will face in school. Each school year students are asked to read more and more. As students are able to organize this information in consistent ways that match the text structures that authors most often use, they will remember the information more effectively. Good readers are able to identify text structures and capture the information contained in the texts they read. Students who can readily spot text structures become much more effective comprehenders of text. The benefits of this strategy will be with students the rest of their lives as they read various types of text. Comparing and identifying text elements is a hallmark of lifelong learners.

Progress Monitoring for the Comparing Text Structures Intervention

This strategy needs frequent checking and progress monitoring. As the teacher, you can use every reading assignment in class as an opportunity to review students' understanding of text structure. You can also work with students in small groups to review the principles and processes for identifying various text structures. While narrative text structures may be easier for students to learn, informational text structures may have a more lasting benefit. As students compare various texts, they will be able to understand better the choices authors make as they write. See how quickly students can identify various text structures (again, Intervention Strategy #4 will help students in this process).

Reading Intervention #3:
Content Inferences

Language is the medium or method through which we understand and convey conceptual knowledge. Understanding how language is organized will help us better understand how knowledge is organized. As students improve their ability to see the organization of written text and the author's intent for writing, they will be able to better recognize the purposes behind their reading and to make meaning from the text. Moats (2000) notes that "comprehension depends, firstly, on a large, working vocabulary and substantial background knowledge" (p. 14). It is important for learners to infer from both oral and written statements. The challenges are much bigger for learners when they engage with written text because formal written text is more academically complex and dense. The differences learners face when inferring from written statements rather than oral statements stem from the fact that writing has much more challenging academic language and much more complex language structures compared to spoken communication. Readers who effectively increase their inferring skills are able to draw accurate conclusions and make sense of the material they read.

A very important bit of research (Nation, 1990) notes that 90 percent of the words that students know, they learned through the process of inferring. Developing the ability to infer may be the single most important factor in becoming an effective learner. Students who have difficulty inferring often struggle as listeners and readers. These students need an intervention that will help them build their inferential abilities.

> **Common Core State Standards**
>
> Grade 4: Refer to details and examples in a text when explaining what the text says explicitly and when **drawing inferences from the text.**
>
> Grade 6: Cite textual evidence to support analysis of what the text says explicitly as well as **inferences drawn from the text.**

What the Content Inferences Intervention Looks Like

Inferring is both a listening and a reading strategy, so it may be best to practice with students using sentences that are either typed out or read to them. Cain & Oakhill (2007) observe, "Children with poor comprehension often fail to generate inferences to go beyond the meanings of individual sentences, to link up ideas within a text, and to incorporate their own background knowledge to make full sense of text" (p. 302). While few students explicitly understand the inferring process, good readers naturally make inferences. As students learn the six types of inferences (Figure 3.5), their reading comprehension will improve dramatically (Johnson, 2009):

Figure 3.5 Six Types of Inferences

- **Infer Location:** The tiny grains of sand wiggled through Susie's toes as she listened to the waves crash against the rocks.
  We might infer Susie is at the beach.
- **Infer Time:** As the full moon shone brightly in the starry sky, the coon dogs began to bark excitedly.
  We might infer it is midnight.
- **Infer Characteristics of an Object:** After scratching all three boxes on the ticket with a quarter, Sandra realized that they all had the same $10,000 amount.
  We might infer that Sandra had a winning lottery ticket.
- **Infer Actions:** The shortstop swung as hard as he could at the pitch; the bat made a loud crack, and the ball flew over the fence.
  We might infer the shortstop hit a homerun.
- **Infer Feelings:** The entire audience gave George a standing ovation for having perfect attendance every day from kindergarten to graduation.
  We might infer that George is feeling pleased or proud.
- **Infer Causal Relationships:** While backing out of the parking spot at the mall, 16-year-old Jennifer heard a loud crunch, and her car stopped suddenly.
  We might infer that Jennifer dented her car's rear bumper.

How the Content Inferences Intervention Works

Consider the following steps for reinforcing this strategy with your students:

1. **Invite students to read content-area sentences** from passages in their science, social studies, mathematics, or language arts textbooks.

2. **Invite students to identify an inference** that they can make from each sentence.

3. **Have students classify the inferences** according to the six types of inferences listed on the chart on page 75.

4. **Ask a student to share his or her answer with the class, explaining** the inference and the classification made.

5. **Ask other students to share a different inference** they made or a different classification they made for an inference.

6. **Point out to students that sentences in various content areas can have multiple inferences,** and inferences can have multiple classifications that make sense and contribute to understanding. (See Figure 3.6.)

7. **Proceed and read other content-area sentences,** stopping at those sentences that provide more than one inference.

8. **Review inference identification and classification** until students can recognize inferences in every content area.

ELL or Struggling Student Scaffolding

Work with struggling students in small groups to review and reinforce their ability to identify and effectively classify inferences according to the six categories. As students gain confidence, invite them to work in pairs with ELL students as they create their own inferences and identify the inferences created by textbook writers or their classroom peers.

Why the Content Inferences Intervention Works

Identifying inferences is a core ability that every student needs to master. Again, the research shows that 90 percent of words that students learn are learned through the process of inferring. Developing this ability is critical to students' confidence as readers and learners. Students' ability to understand science hinges on knowing the difference between observing evidence and making inferences. Science typically values a student's ability to observe the

Figure 3.6 Sample Sentences for Developing Content-Area Inferences

Social Studies Examples

1. The sun shone down on the pyramids that were surrounded by yellow sand as the priests mummified the Pharaoh's body for burial.

2. Lewis & Clark crested the hill and looked down to see Indians digging in the sand on the seashore.

3. Democracy in America began with representatives from each of the thirteen original colonies coming together in the City of Brotherly Love to draft a constitution.

Science Examples

1. The seed was planted in fertile soil, placed near the window, and given the right amount of water.

2. When water evaporates from the earth, what eventually happens to it after it condenses in clouds?

3. When the children arrived at school, the front lawn was wet even though there were no clouds in the sky.

Mathematics Examples

1. If all rectangles have four sides, and all squares have four equal sides, then we can infer that a square is a type of _____.

2. Jamie and Benjamin have 214 stickers altogether. Benjamin and Lupe have 163 stickers altogether. If Lupe has 94 stickers, how many stickers does Jamie have?

3. If a yardstick is three times longer than a ruler, then we can say that the ruler is _____ as long as the yardstick.

Language Arts Examples

1. "The sun moved higher. There was no sign of Ramo. From here I looked down on the harbor and farther on along the coast to the spit that thrust out like a fishhook into the ocean." —*Island of the Blue Dolphins*

2. "His master's calloused hand would rub the great neck and he'd say 'Good Sounder, good Sounder.' In the winter when there were no crops and no pay, fifty cents for a possum and two dollars for a coonhide bought flour and overall jackets with blanket linings." —*Sounder*

3. "I had followed Tom into our big kitchen with its ten-foot-wide coal-burning range. Mamma was kneading dough on the big kitchen table as we entered. I had never seen Mamma's hands idle." —*The Great Brain*

world around us and to cite evidence that supports our understanding of the world. At the same time, many discoveries in science have occurred because scientists made inferences about how and why things happen and then checked these inferences, or hypotheses, by gathering additional evidence. Science is about natural processes that occur in the world. When students understand the academic language transition words and concept words, they better understand how principles of science operate in the world. Once students can recognize inferences in various content areas effectively, they will become much more effective readers. Since 90 percent of new words are learned through the process of inferring, students who are explicitly taught the six types of inferences will be able to create a much richer understanding and clearer picture of the information they are learning.

Progress Monitoring for the Content Area Inferences Intervention

Students can make their own inferences in various content areas and share these with their peers. For example, each student can write five sentences with inferences in several different content areas and then invite their peers to identify the inferences and categorize them according to the six types listed on page 75. Students will enjoy challenging each other, and designing their own inferences in various content areas will demonstrate their ability to understand the inferring process. Teachers should be available to help students who struggle with this activity. Students who have difficulty making inferences will need additional time and attention to develop their confidence in this extremely important area.

Reading Intervention #4:
Signal Words

This strategy is an extension of the text structure strategy addressed in Intervention Strategy #2. This intervention focuses on the words that authors use to signal to readers the types of text structure they are using to convey information. Just as the words "Once upon a time" signal to students that they are about to read a narrative story, other words signal that they are about to read informational text. The signal words outlined in this reading intervention all come from the academic language lists that appear in Appendix A on page 181.

What the Signal Words Intervention Looks Like

This intervention builds confidence for students as they become adept at spotting the signal words that reveal various informational text structures. Signal words are key academic language terms that identify various types of text structure. Pearson (2004) note that "in low income schools, the amount of high level talk about text, challenging assignments, student-centered instruction, and high levels of student engagement predicts growth in student achievement on a variety of measures" (p. 12). Figure 3.7 (adapted from Honig, Diamond, Gutlohn, 2000) outlines several important text structures and the signal words that alert the reader to upcoming patterns for organizing information in the text:

Figure 3.7 Text Structure Types and Signal Words

Text Structure	Signal Words	Message to Reader
Cause/Effect or Problem/Solution	because, due to, since, therefore, so as a result, consequently, nonetheless, if…then, accordingly, thus, nevertheless	These signal words alert the reader to cause(s) leading to effect(s) or problem(s) leading to solutions.
Compare/ Contrast	like, just as, similar, both, also, too, unlike, different, but, in contrast, on the other hand, although, yet, either…or, however, while, as well as, not only…but also, comparatively, likewise, instead	These signal words alert the reader to upcoming comparisons and contrasts.

Continued

Figure 3.7 *Continued*

Text Structure	Signal Words	Message to Reader
Description/ Explanation	moreover, as with most, additionally, in other words, furthermore, second, next, then, finally, most important, also, in fact, significantly, imagine that, for instance, particularly, for example, in front, beside, near	These signal words alert the reader to an upcoming list or set of characteristics.
Sequencing/ Time-Order	before, eventually, first, during, while as, frequently, at the same time, after, initially, whenever, secondly, then, next, at last, finally, now, recently, when, to begin with	These signal words alert the reader to a sequence of events, actions, or steps.

How the Signal Words Intervention Works

1. **Review with students the four different types of informational text structures** covered in Intervention Strategy #2 of this chapter.

2. **Ask students if they would like an easy method for quickly identifying** the text structure the author uses.

3. **Introduce the academic language transition words** that help identify the various text structures.

4. **Organize students into groups** of approximately four students per group.

5. **Provide each group with a different passage,** with each passage representing one of the four informational text structures.

6. **Students in each group should write down the signal words** that reveal the type of informational text structure (e.g., *first, second, eventually, finally* for a time-order text structure).

7. **Once students identify the signal words in their passage, they can exchange passages** with another group and follow the same process of identifying key signal words that reveal the text structure of these other passages.

8. **As a follow-up assignment on another day, students can work in their groups to make posters** of the different types of signal words that reveal informational text structures.

9. **As another follow-up activity, students can be given different colors of Post-it sticky arrows** and use them to identify different signal words that reveal the four types of text structures (e.g., blue for compare/contrast, green for description, yellow for cause/effect, and red for sequential/time-order).

ELL Scaffolding

Ask students to work in pairs with ELL students as they spot signal words or identify text structures. In this way ELLs can ask questions and receive peer support.

Why the Signal Words Intervention Works

This strategy works because it builds tremendous confidence. Students who can quickly identify signal words and the corresponding text structure are able to organize their reading and learning much more effectively. Mastering text structure and being explicitly aware of the type of text structure an author is using is critical to becoming an independent learner. Students who learn to identify signal words are able to better succeed in school, while students who are unable to recognize the common signal patterns used in different structures of text become disengaged with textbooks, learning, and eventually school. The students who never master signal words and text structure become prime candidates for dropping out of school, while students who become proficient in identifying text structure are able to succeed with the increasing complexity of high school and college textbooks.

Progress Monitoring for the Signal Words Intervention

When starting a new chapter in a textbook, invite students to identify the signal words that help identify for the reader the type of text structure that the author is using. Students with frequent practice will become much more proficient at identifying signal words and recognizing text structures. Also ask students which is their favorite type of text structure. Different students enjoy organizing information in their brain differently. Some prefer chronological sequencing, others enjoy cause and effect, some like to compare and contrast, and others get a kick out of descriptive language that paints a picture for the reader. As students evaluate various types of text structure, they will be more attuned to recognizing the different types. The greatest form of progress monitoring may be to have students write short paragraphs about various content area topics according to a specific text structure and use the signal words that reveal these text structures.

Reading Intervention #5: Thinking Aloud

Good readers consistently use strategies that improve their ability to comprehend effectively. These strategies are commonly called cognitive reading strategies because they employ certain cognitive or mental processes that strengthen the reader's comprehension. While some students seem to naturally develop these strategies without any formal instruction, other students need explicit training and practice to develop these reading strategies. Cognitive reading strategies are literacy strategies that enhance the rate at which students can negotiate and transact new information (Olson, 2007). Once students can engage in cognitive reading strategies with fluency and automaticity, they will be able to read any passage more effectively. They will become better comprehenders, and school will make more sense.

Common Core State Standards

Grade 5: Explain the relationships or interactions between two or more individuals, events, ideas, or concepts in a historical, scientific, or technical text based on specific information in the text.

What the Thinking Aloud Intervention Looks Like

Thinking aloud is a modeling approach used by the teacher to reinforce the cognitive reading strategies that students should know and use. In the first book of this series, *RTI Strategies That Work in the K–2 Classroom*, the cognitive reading strategies are explained in detail. While many students who enter the upper primary grades will easily engage in these cognitive reading strategies, many students may still lack these skills. Students in grades 3–6 also need to engage with the cognitive strategies in ways that encourage metacognitive thinking. Thinking aloud gets students to think metacognitively, to think about their thinking, in ways that expand their ability to learn. Hattie (2009) notes that "metacognitive interventions work on self-management learning skills such as planning; monitoring; and where, when, and how to use tactics and strategies" (p. 107). English Language Learners, struggling readers, and students from poverty typically need additional reinforcement to become fully familiar with these strategies. Let's review the list of cognitive reading strategies that research shows are modeled by expert readers.

Cognitive Reading Strategies

- Accessing Prior Knowledge

- Making Predictions

- Visualizing

- Determining Importance

- Generating Questions

- Monitoring and Clarifying

Diehl & Nettles (2010) note that "predicting, connecting, and visualizing are the simplest of the six strategies because they are dependent only upon the reader's prior knowledge" (p. 13). As an expert reader, you should explicitly model and reveal to your students the thinking that goes into these reading strategies.

How the Thinking Aloud Intervention Works

1. **Let students know that you will be consciously "thinking aloud"** about the strategies that help you comprehend when you read.

2. **Select a passage of text and model for students** the types of thinking you do, the types of questions you ask yourself, and the types of clarifying you do to make sure you comprehend effectively.

3. **Each cognitive reading strategy should be "thought aloud"** at various times (e.g., accessing prior knowledge, predicting, visualizing).

4. **Share the conversations that are going on in your head** so that all students can hear what goes on in the head of an expert reader (e.g., "What do I already know about the topic of this passage on Mexico?" or "I predict that the Mexican economy relies on tourism.").

5. **It will take several months of modeling** a variety of reading passages (narrative and informative) for students to internalize the thinking that good readers do.

6. **Once you have modeled for students, pair students up** and have them share their thinking as they read a passage (you may want to pair weaker readers with stronger readers).

7. **After the pairs have worked together, reconvene as a class** and ask students to share their insights and the strategies they used in their reading. (This collective sharing typically provides a robust number of ideas that support good reading strategies.)

8. **For students to internalize the Thinking Aloud Strategy** in their own mind, they will need numerous opportunities to practice as they read.

9. **Have students make posters of the cognitive reading strategies** as well as posters of the examples of thinking out loud that support these strategies.

ELL Scaffolding

Ask students to work in pairs with ELL students to practice thinking aloud. In this way ELLs can ask questions and receive peer support.

Why the Thinking Aloud Intervention Works

Thinking aloud is a strategy where students can use their prior knowledge and imaginations to make a stab at what they will learn. Predicting is an initial step in making inferences. Predictions cause us to make leaps that we believe will help us bridge gaps in the information we are striving to learn. Good readers are constantly making predictions and monitoring, revising, and checking their answers to see if they grow into accurate inferences that bring us closer to a knowledge structure that logically fits together and creates coherent meaning. Poor readers are those who develop only partial or fractured comprehension. Students may recognize the importance of making a prediction or hypothesis before a science experiment, yet do they realize the importance of making a prediction before reading a story or a passage of text. Making and checking predictions are fundamental skills for developing comprehension. As we model for students how to become expert readers, they will begin to internalize the effective reading strategies that will improve their comprehension. This strategy works because it makes explicit the strategies and skills that good readers need. As we think out loud, we reveal to ourselves and others the key reading processes that bolster our comprehension.

Figure 3.8 How Feedback Affects Student Learning

Improvement Results from Teacher Feedback and Student Reflection	Percentile Gain/Loss in Learning
Provide only a right/wrong response	–3%
Provide correct answers to students	+8%
Criteria understood by student vs. not understood	+16%
Correct answers are explained to students	+20%
Students are reassessed until answers are correct	+20%
Students' results are displayed in classroom	+26%
Evaluation has clear expectations (e.g., rubrics, modeling, exemplary samples)	+32%

Progress Monitoring for the Thinking Aloud Intervention

The think-aloud is an easy strategy for progress monitoring. First, you model effective thinking for becoming an expert comprehender. Next, students share their thinking out loud with their peers. Because students will be thinking out loud, the conversations will reveal the level of progress that your students are making. Give students ample opportunities to share their think-aloud. Work with students in small groups if they need additional support. Thinking aloud is a form of feedback for our students. Figure 3.8 above shows how important feedback is for our students.

As students think out loud and ask themselves, "Why did I get this answer correct?" or "What indicates that I definitely know this?" they will be able to reflect effectively on their learning. Students will benefit from knowing how they learn (cognitive strategies) and why they learn (metacognition).

Summing It Up

Developing excellent readers is critical to developing excellent leaders. As readers in our classes learn RTI reading strategies that work, their confidence as learners will increase. This increased confidence will lead to a similar increase in the amount of reading students do and the pleasure with which they read. Guided reading is an effective way to support students while they are reading in small groups. Comparing text structures is a critical ability that we seem to have avoided teaching to our students. Knowing the key signal words will help students identify informational text structures. As our students become adept at identifying text structures, they will become better comprehenders. Inferring is a powerful skill that our students need to learn to become effective listeners, readers, speakers, and writers, yet rarely is it explicitly taught in our classrooms. As students identify and categorize inferences according to the six types listed on page 75, they will increase their cognition and recognition of these words. Thinking aloud reveals our comprehension processes and strengthens our cognitive reading strategies. As all of our students practice these intervention strategies that work, their confidence as readers will increase in powerful ways. They will see lifelong benefits as learners and leaders.

Reflection

1. How effectively do your students infer, and how many types of inferences can they identify?

2. Do your students know the four types of informative text structures, and can they identify the signal words that reveal text structure?

4

Grades 3–6 Math Intervention Strategies

*"The essence of mathematics is not
to make simple things complicated,
but to make complicated things simple."*

—S. Gudder

For Jeremy, math seems like just a jumble of numbers and symbols. When his teacher, Mr. Terwilliger, shows the math on the board it seems to make sense, but once he has a problem in front of him and is working on his own, he admittedly struggles. Fractions are the worst. He is unsure what to do when adding, multiplying, subtracting, or dividing them. Just when he thinks he gets it, he loses the understanding as soon as he has to work a math problem out himself. He does okay on some of his assignments with help from others, but his tests show that he has trouble holding onto concepts. Jeremy's attitude towards math has made the problem worse. He dreads math class and avoids his math homework. His confidence at school is slowly deteriorating. Mr. Terwilliger is concerned, and he knows something needs to be done soon to get things back on track for Jeremy and several other students in class. Jeremy is becoming math-phobic.

Math Interventions

We need to get to the root issue of education, which is quality instruction, rather than attempting to just hack at the leaves of education. The root issue of quality instruction includes targeted interventions that differentiate learning for students with different problems. Many teachers only develop a limited number of strategies in their instructional repertoire to meet the needs of their students (Karen E. Johnson, 2008). It is one thing to be aware that a student needs an intervention. It is crucially essential that instructional capacity is in place so that the student's personal learning needs are met. We have so many students who struggle and need support to help them reach their educational potential. Noting the importance of intervention strategies in math, Van de Walle states,

> For your students to develop effective strategies, you yourself need to have a command of as many good strategies as possible.... The trouble is that far too many students do not develop strategies without instruction and far too many students in middle school continue to count on their fingers. (p. 32)

This chapter will provide strategies for helping students learn multiplication, percentages, fractions, and decimals. For students who are struggling with basic math concepts, we refer you to Chapter 4 in our companion text for the early elementary grades, *RTI Strategies That Work in the K–2 Classroom*.

Engagement

As you have gone through the strategies covered thus far, you may have noticed that they engage learners at deeper levels. Students benefit from learning experiences that feel like a game, challenge them to identify new perspectives, or ask them to organize information in new ways (Stahl & McKenna, 2006). Whether it is the Create-a-Word game, categorizing the six types of inferences, the Academic Language Graphic Organizer, or spotting text-structure signal words, students like to showcase their newfound learning in ways that stretch them. Students like hands-on activities where they get to actively participate in the strategies. The upcoming math intervention strategies encourage students to engage with their classmates and reflect inwardly on their own thinking processes.

Math Processes

In order for students to learn mathematics effectively, we need to teach mathematics as if it were an ill-structured discipline: a domain in which multiple interpretations, argument, and debate are called for and seem natural (Resnick, 1988). When students first start to express their mathematical thinking in words, they often do not use very precise language. Learning to think mathematically requires some mediating processes in order to bridge the gap between students' ordinary language and the language of mathematics. Asking challenging questions consistently can help develop our students' thinking in math. Consider the following questions from Schoenfeld (1987):

- ♦ What (exactly) are you doing?
- ♦ Can you describe it precisely?
- ♦ Why are you doing it?
- ♦ How does it fit into the solution?
- ♦ How does it help you?
- ♦ What will you do with the outcome when you obtain it? (p. 206)

Just as important as the questions we ask students are the questions they ask themselves. Our first strategy provides a plethora of questions that our students can learn to ask as they engage in math. Let's get started.

Math Intervention #1: Questioning Aloud

In many ways, math in the elementary grades is taught as calculations that students do in their mind. Questioning aloud gets students to say out loud the questions that they are thinking. Students benefit when they communicate their metacognitive processes out loud. In addition, this strategy adds quality questions to your students' repertoire of mathematics thinking. Whether students are adding, subtracting, multiplying, or dividing or are working with fractions, decimals, or story problems, the question aloud strategy helps students engage more deeply in the math processes. According to Kerry (1982), teachers ask approximately 1000 questions per week. How many questions do students ask themselves as they engage in learning new material? Consider the following reasons for students to ask questions of themselves or their peers in math class (adapted from http://www.musk ingum.edu/~cal/database/general/questioning.html):

- to identify misconceptions
- to evaluate learning
- to guide thinking
- to encourage engagement of learners
- to diagnose strengths and weaknesses
- to help students form the habit of reflection
- to help students learn to construct meaning
- to summarize information
- to relate concepts together

As our students ask effective questions while they perform basic math operations in grades 3–6, they will understand the math more robustly and they will be better prepared to understand math when it becomes more abstract in middle school and high school.

Common Core State Standards

Grade 3: Ask questions to check understanding of information presented, stay on topic, and link their comments to the remarks of others.

Grade 4: Organize, represent, and interpret data with up to three categories; ask and answer questions about the total number of data points, how many in each category, and how many more or less are in one category than in another.

What the Questioning Aloud Intervention Looks Like

As our students verbalize their thinking and ask questions that promote thinking, they will learn more. Developing a variety of strategies that promote math thinking and math literacy will strengthen student understanding (Kenney, Hancewicz, Heuer, Metisto, & Tuttle, 2005). This strategy works to expand both the number and the quality of questions our students ask themselves as they engage in their math assignments. Students who do well in math ask questions naturally. The National Council of Teachers of Mathematics (NCTM, 2000) emphasizes the importance of effective communication in math: Reflection and communication are intertwined processes in mathematics learning (p. 61). Struggling math students need examples and practice in asking and answering a variety of questions. Simply stated, asking questions is an effective way to learn (Van de Walle, 2004). Consider the following list to help your students ask more questions while they do their math classwork (adapted from PBS's Teacherline: http://www.pbs.org/teachers/_files/pdf/Microsoft%20Word_FINALMathTipDoc.pdf).

Question Aloud Guiding Questions

To help students build confidence and rely on their own understanding, get them to ask…

- Why is that true?
- How did I reach that conclusion?
- Does that make sense?
- Can I make a model to show that?

To help students learn to reason mathematically, get them to ask…

- Is that true for all cases? Explain.
- Can I think of opposite examples (or non-examples)?
- How would I prove that?
- What assumptions am I making?

To check student progress, get them to ask…

- Can I explain what _____ has done so far? What else is there to do?
- Why did I decide to use this method?
- Can I think of another method that might have worked?
- Is there a more efficient strategy?
- What do I notice when…?
- Why did I decide to organize my results like that?
- Do I think this would work with other numbers?
- Have I thought of all the possibilities? How can I be sure?

To help students collectively make sense of mathematics, get them to ask…

- What do I think about what _____ said?
- Do I agree? Why or why not?
- Does anyone have the same answer but a different way to explain it?

- Do I understand what ____ is saying?
- Can I convince the rest of the group that the answer makes sense?

To encourage conjecturing, get them to ask…

- What would happen if…? What if not?
- Do I see a pattern? Can I explain the pattern?
- What are some possibilities here?
- Can I predict the next one? What about the last one?
- What other questions would I add to this list?

To promote problem solving, get them to ask…

- What do I need to find out?
- What information do I have?
- What strategies am I going to use?
- Will I figure out the problem mentally? With pencil and paper? Using a number line?
- Will a calculator help?
- What tools will I need?
- What do I think the answer or result will be?

To help when students get stuck, get them to ask…

- How would I describe the problem in my own words?
- What do I know what is not stated in the problem?
- What facts do I have?
- How did I tackle similar problems?
- Could I try it with simpler numbers? Fewer numbers? Using a number line?
- What about putting things in order?
- Would it help to create a diagram? Make a table? Draw a picture?
- Can I guess and check?
- Have I compared my work to anyone else's? What did other members of my group try?

To make connections among ideas and applications, get them to ask…

- How does this relate to …?
- What ideas that we learned previously were useful in solving this problem?

- What uses of mathematics did I find in the newspaper last night?
- Can I see an example of _____ in the classroom?

To encourage reflection, get them to ask…

- How did I get the answer?
- Does my answer seem reasonable? Why or why not?
- Can I describe this method to the class? Can I explain why it works?
- What if I had started with _____ rather than _____ ?
- What if I could only use _____ ?
- What have I learned or found out today?
- Did I use or learn any new words today? What do they mean? How do you spell them?
- What are the key points or big ideas in this lesson?
- What other questions would I add to this list?

In addition to the previous examples of questions, students can craft their own lists of guiding questions to help them get through different math operations. For example, students can create guiding questions for math functions like adding fractions, dividing decimals, or multiplying percentages.

How the Questioning Aloud Intervention Works

1. **Ask students to work in small groups of three or four** and have them review the questions they will be sharing out loud.

2. **Give students poster paper and color markers** so that they can make a poster of the various types of questions that support math thinking.

3. **Ask students to make a poster** using at least four colors, listing the questions so that the class can see them easily and making sure there is a border for the poster.

4. **Display the posters on the wall** for student reference and support.

5. **Ask students to ask themselves the questions on the posters** as they learn their math.

6. **If students struggle, they should ask a peer** these questions before they ask the teacher for help.

7. **Ask students to write down the information from the posters** on 4 x 6 note cards for personal use or to use as reference guides for homework.

8. **Students can use the posters and the note cards** to help guide the questions they ask to develop their math thinking.

9. **Invite students to ask at least three questions** when they approach new math equations.

10. **After students have asked themselves and peers questions,** they can ask the teacher for assistance if they still need help.

Why the Questioning Aloud Intervention Works

This intervention works because it can be used with any mathematical concept, from addition to algebra. Helping students realize that analyzing information or patterns and then asking effective questions is an important part of mathematical thinking. Questions affect our students' achievement and their attitude towards learning. Students who ask lots of questions are more engaged in the learning that occurs in the classroom. The quantity of questions students ask coincides with the quantity of thinking they do. A big advantage of question aloud strategies is that they are flexible and cover a lot of math situations. Students benefit when they ask themselves lots of questions. Expert learners are typically expert questioners. Students like engaging with their peers, challenging them with questions, and being challenged in return.

Progress Monitoring for the Questioning Aloud Intervention

Before questioning students about how they are doing with their math, ask them to share the questions that they have asked themselves. Have students, when they go to the board and do math in front of the class, share aloud the questions that they are thinking in their mind. Ask students to write 3–5 questions at the bottom of their homework paper with the types of questions they are asking themselves, and then discuss some of these questions in class. Students can pair up with a classmate and take turns asking questions. This can raise the quality of questions as students do their math and think of new ways for determining a solution. Listen to the quantity and quality of questions students ask aloud as they work in pairs. Students like to work in pairs to do math and ask questions out loud.

Math Intervention #2:
Estimating Conversations

Estimating is the mathematical process of guessing the approximate value of a number. The process of estimating is helpful when an approximate value provides a sufficient answer or the precise value is difficult to determine. As students focus on the methods that they use to estimate, their confidence with math will increase. Estimations work well for grades 3–6 students when they are measuring, counting, or computing equations (Van de Walle, 2004). Consider the following list as a reminder:

Three Areas for Estimating

♦ **Measurement estimation**: How many feet long is the classroom?

♦ **Quantity estimation**: How many jelly beans are in the jar?

♦ **Computational estimation**: Is 9×11 close to 10×10 or 100?

It is important to support everyone's best guess or estimation while taking the time to verbalize the type of reasoning that will help students arrive at more accurate estimations. The process of estimating is a risk-taking effort, and some students will need encouragement. Measurement and quantity estimations involve reasoning and number sense. Nearly all computational estimation involves using easier-to-use parts of numbers like five counts, ten counts, and 100 counts. Computational estimations are also helpful to check if an answer is reasonable.

Common Core State Standards

Grade 3: Measure and estimate liquid volumes and masses of objects using standard units of grams (g), kilograms (kg), and liters (l). Add, subtract, multiply, or divide to solve one-step word problems involving masses or volumes that are given in the same units, e.g., by using drawings (such as a beaker with a measurement scale) to represent the problem.

What the Estimating Conversations Intervention Looks Like

Conversations about estimating involve reasonable guesses that include discussions with a classmate where students share their reasoning processes and articulate their understanding. Most importantly, students must be able to explain the reasoning behind their estimation processes. According to Rubenstein (2001), "when students have regular opportunities to estimate, share orally, evaluate, compare their approaches, and transfer strategies to new settings, they feel challenged, and, ultimately empowered" (p. 443).

While students typically use one of the three following estimating strategies, they should be encouraged to use any ideas they can think of to support their estimations. Here are three common types of estimating strategies that will help students arrive at effective estimates:

Types of Estimating Strategies

+ **Eyeball Estimates:** (e.g., The classroom is 50 feet long.) This estimating strategy involves an educated guess and an understanding of units of measurement.

+ **Sampling Estimates:** (e.g., The heart beats 7,200 times a day.) This estimating strategy involves a sample like "my heart beats 50 times a minutes, so I estimate a heart beats approximately 7,200 times a day (50 beats × 60 minutes × 24 hours)."

+ **Analysis Estimates:** (e.g., The cost of a birthday party with 12 guests will be $76.) This estimating strategy involves performing a variety of calculations to arrive at an approximate amount. The following spreadsheet method of estimating can also help prepare students for algebraic equations.

Party Supplies	Quantity	Unit Cost	Total Cost
2 liters of soda	4	$ 1.75	$ 7.00
Pizzas	3	$15.00	$45.00
Treat bag	12	$ 2.00	$24.00
		Estimated Cost:	$76.00

All three of the estimating strategies involve some form of reasoning rather than outright guessing. The analysis estimating strategy coupled with the spreadsheet can also be used to transition students to basic algebra concepts. Omit one of the parts of the equation and then ask students to solve it. Students can run the calculations to arrive at the unknown quantity. Teachers should first model "estimating talk" as they are going through the math operations to demonstrate the reasoning they use to make an educated or calculated guess. Eventually ask students to engage in talk-aloud processes with their classmates. Use real examples when practicing estimation. The following real-world ideas can help students have fun with estimating.

+ Grocery shopping costs

+ Number of kids in the school

+ Planning a trip and expenses

+ Length of the school hallway

- How many time a year students need to get a haircut

- Area of lawn mown and time it will take to mow

- How many students fit on a school bus

- Average number of TV hours watched per week

- Number of steps it takes to get to the office

- How much it would cost to go to a sporting event (tickets, parking, snacks, gas, and so forth)

Estimations can also be used with any number of combinations of math operations, including fractions (e.g., estimate $3\frac{1}{3}$ meters added to $4\frac{3}{4}$ meters), multiplication, subtraction, addition, division, decimals, and percentages.

How the Estimating Conversations Intervention Works

1. **Explain the concept of estimating to students** and give examples of when estimating may be helpful (e.g., How many candy bars can you get at the mini-mart with $3.00?).

2. **Instruct students on the three areas of estimating** (measurement, quantity, and computational), and make sure they can explain the difference.

3. **Provide students with a few estimating equations** that require them to use estimated measurements, quantity, and computations, and ask them to discuss with their friends how they made their estimations.

4. **Instruct students on the three types of estimating strategies** (eyeball, sampling, and analysis), and make sure they realize all three use calculations rather than random guesses.

5. **Provide pairs of students with additional estimating equations** and ask them to explain to their partner their estimate and how they arrived at this estimate.

6. **Ask volunteers to share with the class** the strategies they used to arrive at their estimates. (It is important that all students feel confident about their estimating skills.)

7. **After students gain confidence with estimating whole numbers**, ask them to make estimates using fractions, decimals, or percentages.

8. **You can play the Range-Finder game** similar to the one in *The Price Is Right*, and ask students to provide a range of answers that are close.

Why the Estimating Conversations Intervention Works

Math is much more fun when students can do a pair-share and talk to their partner as they work on their math. Vary partners so that strong students can work with and model skills for students who may need extra support to process the math efficiently. The brain loves to estimate and predict (Rock, 2009). The key is for students learn to estimate effectively. Encourage students to follow through and check their estimates with the final answer. Checking for correct answers is an important process in math. Learning to estimate answers before beginning a math operation is important in helping students verify that they understand both the answer and the processes used to get to the answer.

Progress Monitoring for the Estimating Conversations Intervention

Many students who struggle with math may also struggle with making estimates. Help these students narrow down the choices they have so that they can start to focus their thinking. For example, the following scaffolds can be used for students who need help with estimating:

1. **More or less than** _____?
2. **Closer to** _____ **or** _____?
3. **About how many (units)** _____?

The third question provides the students with a standard unit of measurement to use in calculating their estimations. It is also helpful to give students estimating situations that use the same unit of measurement so students can start to see patterns and common comparisons. If students are reluctant to pinpoint their best risk-taking calculation, ask them to give a range of estimates. This range of estimates can be a lot like *The Price Is Right* game show on network TV.

Math Intervention #3: Fabulous Fractions

Fractions help students start to see that whole numbers can be broken down into smaller portions. Fractions can be challenging for students to learn because of the transition from whole numbers to parts of numbers that occurs at this level of math education. The idea of considering fractional parts or shares of a whole integer or whole shape is conceptually complex. Fractions are a difficult concept for students to grasp because they are abstract and the notion of the "next" number does not exist (since between any two fractions is another fraction). The ability to compute fractions is a skill that is widely used in the real world. Van de Walle (2006) notes, "fractions have always represented considerable challenge for students, even into the middle grades" (p. 293). Fractions represent a share of a whole, and students in grades 3–6 are highly conscious of sharing fairly.

Common Core State Standards

Grade 3: Explain equivalence of fractions in special cases, and compare fractions by reasoning about their size.

♦ Understand two fractions as equivalent (equal) if they are the same size, or the same point on a number line.

♦ Recognize and generate simple equivalent fractions, e.g., 1/2 = 2/4, 4/6 = 2/3. Explain why the fractions are equivalent, e.g., by using a visual fraction model.

What the Fabulous Fractions Intervention Looks Like

Fractions are best introduced to students by showing them that fractions are all about "fair share." If we take a whole pie, orange, or pizza, how would we cut it to make sure each person receives a fair share if there are two people, three people, four people, five people, and so on? Empson and Levi (2011) note that the most effective way to introduce fractions is through a "fair share" approach where everyone gets an equal share. For example, six kids want to share a four-foot submarine sandwich. If each kid receives a fair share, how many feet of sandwich will each receive? Start with the whole, and then work down to smaller and larger fractions. Make sure that students can identify the proper vocabulary for each fraction they encounter and communicate those terms, such as halves, thirds, fourths, fifths, sixths, sevenths, eighths, ninths, tenths, elevenths, and so forth. According to *The Final Report of the National Math Panel* (2008), "The teaching of fractions must be acknowledged as critically important and improved before an increase in student achievement in algebra can be expected" (p. 18).

Consider the following approaches and perspectives for intervening when students struggle to learn fractions:

♦ Fractional parts are equal shares or equal sized portions of a whole or a unit.

♦ Fractional parts have special names (e.g., halves, fourths, eighths).

♦ The more fractional parts it takes to make a whole, the smaller each part.

♦ The top number tells how many of the fractional parts.

♦ Fractions can be viewed as portions of a number line.

♦ The bottom number identifies the kind of fractional part.

♦ Fractions can be divisors of whole numbers (e.g., one-fourth can divide into a whole number four times).

♦ Two equivalent fractions are two ways of describing the same amount (e.g., one-half, two-fourths, and eight-sixteenths).

Consider using the following fraction chants (Figure 4.1) to provide students with a quick reminder of the important aspects of adding, subtraction, multiplying, and dividing fractions (Susan Winebrenner, 1996).

The teaching of fractions works well for students when they make the connection to fractions of a whole, to decimals of a whole, and to percentages of a whole. For example, students in grades 3–6 need to know that ¼ of a whole circle is the same as .25 of a whole circle and 25% of a whole circle. The meanings of operations on fractions are the same as for whole numbers. The top number is the counting number; it tells the number of parts. The bottom number tells what is being counted or the type of part.

How the Fabulous Fractions Intervention Works

1. **Explain that fractions are part of a whole** and are expressed one number (numerator) over another number (denominator) to show the portion of a whole.

Figure 4.1 Fraction Chants

Adding Fractions	Subtracting Fractions
Adding fractions is my game When the bottom numbers are the same. $\dfrac{3}{6} + \dfrac{2}{6} = \dfrac{5}{6}$	Subtracting fractions—I'm all grins! But bottom numbers must be twins! $\dfrac{3}{4} - \dfrac{1}{4} = \dfrac{2}{4}$ or $\dfrac{1}{2}$
Multiplying Fractions	**Dividing Fractions**
Multiplying fractions is no problem, You take the top times the top and the bottom times the bottom. $\dfrac{2}{3} \times \dfrac{1}{5} = \dfrac{2}{15}$	Dividing fractions is our cry. Just invert the second and multiply. $\dfrac{2}{3} \div \dfrac{3}{4} = \dfrac{2}{3} \times \dfrac{4}{3} = \dfrac{8}{9}$

2. **Demonstrate the "Fair Share" approach to explain fractions** by dividing something kids might share, like a whole pie, pizza, or apple.

3. **Explain that when the numerator is larger than the denominator,** you have at least one whole plus a fraction.

4. **Use tangible objects and have students fill in a portion of the object** (e.g., rectangles, circles, fraction strips, number lines) to identify the fractional portion requested (e.g., 1/4, 3/5, 2/3).

5. **Share the fraction chants, and invite students to create** their own chants to explain different aspects of fractions.

ELL Scaffolding

Use fraction flash cards and have students say fractions out loud to show their understanding, or have them compute (add, subtract, or multiply) simple fractions to see how fluent ELL students are.

Why the Fabulous Fractions Intervention Works

This strategy works because students will be more engaged when they use the Fair Share approach to fractions. Once students recognize that fractions are a portion of a whole, they will be able to more easily grasp adding, subtracting, multiplying, and dividing fractions. Students in grades 3–6 are often focused on fairness, and teaching a strategy that makes sure everyone receives an equal share is a good way to grab their attention and help them understand the basic concept of fractions of a whole.

Progress Monitoring for the Fabulous Fractions Intervention

Work with students in small groups to determine their ability to add, subtract, multiply, and divide fractions effectively. As you work with small groups of students, ask them to turn to their group neighbor and explain how they computed or solved the fraction equations. Listen carefully to students to see if they are able to explain what they did. Also, students should be able to explain a basic fraction in terms of a percentage or a decimal amount of a whole. Use real fruit (oranges) and tangible shapes (circles, squares) that students can cut up to see the portions. You can also talk about fractional portions of the class. For example you can ask one-fourth of the class to go to each of the four sides of the room. After the students figure out how to do this, have students who struggle explain how it was computed. Use whiteboards to have students show their work or write out the explanations to their math work. Ultimately, struggling students should be able to show and say how they arrived at a correct answer to demonstrate they have fully learned important fraction concepts.

Math Intervention #4:
Measurement/Geometry Shapes

We are realizing through research and classroom practice that areas often considered higher math concepts, like algebra and geometry, need to be introduced much sooner to elementary students. When students in grades 3–6 understand basic geometry concepts, they will be much more likely to succeed in high school math. Geometric mathematics studies two-dimensional and three-dimensional objects. Students need to learn many vocabulary terms (Figure 4.2) to understand this area of mathematics. Geometry at the most basic level involves measurement of shapes, angles, and so forth. Measurement involves a comparison of one item with a unit of measurement (e.g.,

Figure 4.2 Sample Measurement Terms

Length	Volume (Capacity)	Degrees
inch	gallon	angle
foot	quart	Celsius
yard	pint	temperature
mile	cup	Fahrenheit
meter	fluid ounce	temperature
centimeter	liter	
kilometer	milliliter	
millimeter	kiloliter	

inch, foot, or yard.) For example, a foot-long hot dog compared to an inch is a 1:12 comparison. (This can also introduce the concept of ratios.) So, the initial understanding of geometry involves clear comprehension of measuring and the vocabulary of units of measurement. Students should consider measurement from a variety of perspectives, like length, volume, and time.

Students' understanding of math will benefit when students know that there are different degrees of measurement.

Common Core State Standards

Grade 3: Recognize area as an attribute of plane figures and understand concepts of area measurement.

♦ A square with side length 1 unit, called "a unit square," is said to have "one square unit" of area, and can be used to measure area.

♦ A plane figure which can be covered without gaps or overlaps by n unit squares is said to have an area of n square units.

Grade 3: Measure areas by counting unit squares (square cm, square m, square in, square ft, and improvised units).

What the Measurement/Geometry Shapes Intervention Looks Like

Measurement is a very practical activity for putting our students' basic math skills—like number sense, adding, and subtracting—to work. Meaningful measurement and estimation depend on familiarity with the unit (e.g., ruler, paper clips). This is why students use tangible units they can understand in context. Area and volume formulas provide a method of measuring these attributes by using only measures of length. Key concepts in geometry that students can measure or check are listed below:

Key Concepts in Geometry

- Point

- Line

- Plane

- Length

- Width

- Height

- Volume

- Angle

- Congruence

- Right Angle

The following ideas can help assist our students as they develop their knowledge of measuring and basic geometry (adapted from Charlesworth, 2011):

- Create mental images of geometric shapes.

- Recognize and represent shapes from different perspectives.

- Relate ideas in geometry to ideas in number and measurement.

- Recognize geometric shapes and structures in the environment.

- Recognize the attributes of length, volume, weight, area, and time.

- Compare and order objects according to these attributes.

- Understand how to measure using nonstandard and standard units.

- Select an appropriate unit and tool for the attribute being measured.

- Measure with multiple copies of units of the same size, such as paper clips laid end to end.

- Use repetition of a single unit to measure something larger than the unit.

- Use tools to measure.

- Develop common referents for measurements to make comparisons and estimates.

- Pose questions and gather data about themselves and their surroundings.

- Sort and classify objects according to their attributes.

- Represent data using concrete objects, pictures, and graphs.

- Describe parts of the data and the set of data as a whole to determine what the data show.

So now that we have some initial ideas, let's look at more ways for developing our students' understanding of measurement and geometry.

How the Measurement/Geometry Shapes Intervention Works

This intervention, like others, involves consistent instruction and practice over the course of time. This section will outline several of the important processes for measuring and learning geometric shapes.

1. **Introduce the concept of measurement,** which is comparing an item to a unit used to measure.

2. **Invite students to think of different units of measurement** (e.g., size, weight, temperature).

3. **Introduce the key vocabulary words for geometry** and measurement. Make sure students understand the words. (They can use the academic language graphic organizer in Chapter 2 to develop their vocabulary.)

4. **Ask students to work in pairs to find several items in the classroom that match the different geometry vocabulary** (e.g., point, line, height, plane). Finding these items will demonstrate and reveal the students' level of understanding.

5. **Ask students to find several items in the classroom to measure** and determine the unit of measurement they choose. Then have them measure and compare their results among items.

6. **Have students discuss with a partner their understanding of measuring geometric shapes,** and then engage in a class discussion regarding the insights they gained.

7. **For larger units of measurement, ask students to go out on the playground and find geometric shapes** to measure, like the merry-go-round, four-square court, or monkey bars, and have them measure and identify the shapes.

8. **On another occasion, after introducing the concept of degrees, have students measure the degrees of angles** and find right angles from objects in the classroom or on the playground.

9. **Have students cut out geometric shapes and match angles**, particularly right angles, for shapes such as squares, rectangles, and triangles.

Why the Measurement/Geometry Shapes Intervention Works

This strategy or combination of strategies works because students have to identify geometric shapes and measurement vocabulary. Students' understanding will grow as they locate real items that surround them every day. This intervention is a great way for students to use basic math (measuring, counting, adding, and subtracting) in practical ways while also building a great foundation for the grander geometry concepts they will learn in middle and high school. As students analyze and measure various geometric shapes, they will be using math while also increasing their awareness of the world around them.

Progress Monitoring for the Measurement/Geometry Shapes Intervention

Invite students to show how they arrived at their answers. Measurement and geometry lend themselves very easily to checking and verifying. Have students work with a partner to confirm their thinking and answers. Students who struggle with basic geometry patterns benefit from measuring length, height, width, and angles of various shapes. Grades 3–6 students should be able to translate units of measurement between inches and feet, so check and make sure each student can translate units of measurement. Give students measuring tools and various geometric cutouts so that students can see the shapes as they demonstrate their understanding of geometric principles. Again, asking students to identify geometric shapes and measure actual objects in the classroom is highly engaging for students, and you can check their progress easily.

Math Intervention #5:
Algebra Fundamentals

Algebra has become the standard requirement for many eighth graders across the nation, and it is a significant barrier that leads to drop-outs. Algebraic thinking encourages students to identify patterns, make number generalizations, and use symbols to take the place of variable numbers. Mathematics and particularly algebra is the science of pattern and order. Algebra includes thinking that involves patterns, generalizations, and relationships (Shoenfeld, 1992).

Algebraic Thinking

- Identifying patterns

- Making number generalizations

- Using symbols to quantify relationships (p. 334)

Common Core State Standards

Grade 6: Solve real-world and mathematical problems by writing and solving equations of the form $x + p = q$ and $px = q$ for cases in which p, q and x are all nonnegative rational numbers.

What the Algebra Fundamentals Intervention Looks Like

Algebra uses symbolic representation (e.g., a = b + c) to help students understand equations

The following algebraic concepts are important for students to grasp in the elementary grades:

- Patterns

- Relationships

- Variables

- Equality

- Constants

- Change

Variables: These numbers represent unknown values or a range of values. Word equations (commonly known as word problems) can help students construct math examples that help them see how changing the number of friends invited to a party affects the total cost for hamburgers. A function table (Figure 4.3) can help students see how the variables result in different costs. Figure 4.4 shows a growing cornstalk example.

Figure 4.3 Function Table

Number of Friends at Party	Average Number of Hamburgers	Total Cost for Hamburgers
1	2	$ 3.00
3	6	$ 9.00
5	10	$15.00
7	14	$21.00
9	18	$24.00

Cost = Friends (a) × 2 × 1.50

Figure 4.4 Stalk Height by Week

Week	Height (inches)
1	3
2	4
3	5
4	6

Stalk height = week (a) +2 inches

Equality: The equal sign represents balance or equivalence and can be expressed in a variety of ways. Consider different ways to express the same equation involving the weight of a cantaloupe compared to that of a peach.

Cantaloupe weight = peach weight + peach weight + peach weight

Cantaloupe weight = (3) × peach weight

Cantaloupe weight / 3 = peach weight

Constants: In algebra, a constant is a number that does not change. In the equation for converting Fahrenheit to Celsius, the numbers 1.8 and 32 are constants.

Fahrenheit = Celsius × 1.8 + 32

At the same time as the numbers for Fahrenheit vary (variable), the Celsius numbers will also vary.

Change: Algebra also helps us identify the rate of change, like how fast we grow each year, how fast the school bus travels, or how long it takes the merry-go-round to slow down when it is spinning at its fastest.

The skills outlined in the next how-to section should be interspersed throughout the school year to support algebraic thinking. It will typically take students repeated efforts to grasp the relationships among these concepts.

How the Algebra Fundamentals Intervention Works

1. **Instruct students on the various types of algebraic terminology** (e.g., variables, constants, change).

2. **Invite students to identify patterns in the world around them** (e.g., weather patterns: how many degrees difference each day is there in a week; color patterns: how many kids have on blue shirts; or interval patterns: how long is it between breaks or recess).

3. **Have students come up with a symbol for a variable** in a simple equation. Typically we use the letter a to represent an unknown. Asking students to label the symbol will help them connect and identify with the unknown variable (e.g., If Q + 3 = 5, then the answer for Q is 2.).

4. **Ask students to identify a range of variables** in the world around them (e.g., How long it takes students to run the 100 yard dash, How many steps does it take to get to the pencil sharpener or bathroom, How quickly can students be quiet when asked by the teacher).

5. **Invite students to determine the difference between a constant and a variable** (e.g., number of students in a class compared to how many bring a sack lunch on a given day).

6. **Direct students to make a function table for a party,** and have them decide on the menu and approximate cost.

7. **Help students see that basic math computational skills will help them solve equations that involve algebraic thinking.**

8. **Have fun with students as they creatively determine unknown** or abstract quantities; be patient with their progress.

ELL Scaffolding

Ask students to work in pairs with ELL students as they answer questions or solve algebraic equations.

Why the Algebra Fundamentals Intervention Works

This intervention works because it breaks down the key components of algebraic equations. Algebra is all about skills like identifying variables and quantities, determining rate of change, recognizing patterns, and noting constants. Being aware of these concepts and knowing the terminology that describes them will help students begin to think algebraically. Students need algebra skills to succeed in middle school and high school. Building an effective foundation is important for all students. Algebra may be the biggest math challenge that students are required to face in their academic careers. Students who can overcome this challenge walk through a gateway that opens up future college and career opportunities.

Progress Monitoring for the Algebra Fundamentals Intervention

Check to see if students can fill in information that is missing where they need to reason abstractly to arrive at an answer. The key to progress monitoring for Algebra Fundamentals is to make sure students can identify missing information. Word problems often involve a lot of algebraic thinking to solve the equation. This is one of the reasons that word problems can be so challenging for students. Check to see if students use the algebraic terminology accurately. Knowing what a variable, constant, equality, and rate of change are is important to eventually identifying this information. Algebraic thinking requires abstract thinking, so be patient with students who struggle thinking abstractly. Students will benefit in middle school because they have been introduced to the key terminology and concepts that comprise algebra. As long as students are able to grasp basic equations dealing with constants, variables, and change, they will be on the right track.

Summing It Up

Math interventions in grades 3–6 need to help students gain confidence in their ability to reason and interact with numbers. Students who have success in math ask effective questions as they think and reason. They use a variety of estimating strategies, they can think abstractly algebraically, and they are aware of geometric shapes and measuring different shapes. Struggling students typically need additional attention, time, and small-group instruction to strengthen their math strategies. The questioning aloud strategy gets students to question and reason as they do math, and it expands the quality of the questions they ask themselves. The estimating conversations strategy encourages students to make estimates as they solve equations and explain their reasoning through conversations with their peers. The measuring/geometry strategy expects students to measure practical everyday things that surround them and to notice how geometric shapes construct the world around us. The algebra fundamentals strategy introduces students to the vocabulary, concepts, and ideas that will help them think abstractly and solve for unknown quantities. As your students more fully develop their math skills and strategies, they will become more confident and more engaged in math and see the real-world benefits for understanding math.

Reflection

1. What questions do your students ask themselves as they face challenging math equations?
2. How do students who struggle in your class explain mathematical processes involved in estimation?

5

Grades 3–6 Speaking Intervention Strategies

*"The liberty of speaking
and writing guards
our other liberties."*

—Thomas Jefferson

As Juanita waits for the school bus, she smells the blossoms from the almond orchards that surround her house. Her family moved many times during her first couple of years in school. Fortunately they have stayed in their current home for over a year now. Juanita feels bashful, and at school she says as little as possible. She can speak English casually with her classmates, but she has spoken so little in class her teacher is unsure what to do. In class, Juanita nods her head or quietly gives one word answers whenever anyone speaks to her. She is well behaved and typically goes unnoticed by her teacher who is busy with a large class. With so many English Language Learners at her school, being quiet is a good strategy to stay under the radar. Unfortunately, it is also a strategy that limits her opportunity to practice speaking English. Juanita is an infrequent speaker who is stalled at the intermediate level of English Language Development.

Speaking Confidence

Teaching speaking strategies as a response to intervention makes sense on many levels. Students receive tremendous benefits when they receive multiple opportunities to speak in class. Through the process of speaking in class, our students reveal their thinking processes to others as well as themselves. When they speak, they also engage more with classroom content and new information. They benefit as they negotiate meaning and participate in content-area conversations. Because meaning is a negotiated process, for students to make meaning, they need to be given situations where they can discuss their understanding and thinking in a variety of settings. As instructional leaders in the classroom, we should integrate a variety of speaking strategies in large-group, small-group, and paired-partner activities. The strategies should be able to meet the needs of all students and provide particular support to our socioeconomically disadvantaged students, English Language Learners, and struggling learners.

Making Meaning

We make meaning out of the world around us. This involves prior knowledge, context, and a variety of other factors. Meaning making is a negotiated process. Students who lack essential grade 3–6 level vocabulary (especially ELLs and low socioeconomic students) struggle to consistently make meaning of the content they are expected to learn. These students need ample opportunities to receive input they can comprehend and to communicate meaningful output to others. The strategies in this section are specifically designed to support content learning in key academic areas. Wolfram et al. (1999) note, "All children need linguistically rich classrooms in all subject areas to develop expertise in literacy and academic talk, the genre of language used in teaching and learning, and in business and professional settings" (p. 126). Speaking abilities are part of what constitutes a literate person in our increasingly competitive world. Speaking is important in working as a team member in a collaborative fashion. Speaking helps students develop the communication patterns that are part of a professional discourse that is different from what they are accustomed to. In addition to communicating actively with others, students will strengthen their confidence as they are able to express themselves effectively.

Academic Literacy and Struggling Students

The increasing number of English Language Learners in our schools has brought extra challenges to the issues of poverty that already exist. Finding lasting solutions for these students requires that educators to take a more in-depth look at language and literacy. Many African American students, Hispanic students, and students who face poverty struggle in school. As educators, we can understand some of the challenges that English Language Learners face, yet the struggles that African American students experience may often be more difficult to grasp. When educators and students look more closely at their casual word and language patterns, the answers become more evident. While addressing the use of street vernacular used by many African American youth, the comedian Bill Cosby (Cosby and Poussaint, 2007) says, "Let's face it—the high dropout rate for black students is related in part to poorly developed language skills, and this shortcoming keeps getting bigger and bigger over the years." These statements may be extreme, yet they do emphasize the importance of language in the school environment. While many students lack the ability to speak Standard English effectively, we should respect our students' casual and home language.

Speaking and ELLs

Speaking may be the biggest challenge for English Language Learners. These students often avoid speaking in class (e.g., asking questions, answering the teacher, speaking out loud) because they lack confidence. Yet the students who may avoid engaging in class conversations are those who most need to take advantage of speaking in English. Many ELLs in grades 3–6 speak only their native language in the comforts of home, so it is vital that they are provided ample opportunities to speak in English at school. The expectations of the national Teachers of English of Speakers of Other Languages highlight the importance of developing speaking skills, particularly for ELLs.

TESOL Standards

Goal 1: To use English to communicate in social settings

    Standard 1: Students will use English to participate in social interactions.

    Standard 2: Students will interact in, through, and with spoken and written English for personal expression and enjoyment.

    Standard 3: Students will use learning strategies to extend their communicative competence.

Continued

> **Goal 2: To use English to achieve academically in all content areas**
>
> **Standard 1:** Students will use English to interact in the classroom.
>
> **Standard 2:** Students will use English to obtain, process, construct, and provide subject-matter information in spoken and written form.
>
> **Standard 3:** Students will use appropriate learning strategies to construct and apply academic knowledge.
>
> **Goal 3: To use English in socially and culturally appropriate ways:**
>
> **Standard 1:** Students will use the appropriate language variety, register, and genre according to audience, purpose, and setting.
>
> **Standard 2:** Students will use appropriate learning strategies to extend their sociolinguistic and cultural competence.

As students master the following interventions, they will achieve the Common Core State Standards as well as the TESOL Standards that are such a large part of academic success. Students who struggle to speak effectively often struggle to become effective writers (Johnson & Johnson, 2006). Let's jump into the speaking strategies.

Speaking Intervention #1: Informational Storytelling

Everyone likes hearing a story, and students especially like curling up on the rug to listen to the teacher. Students also like to share stories that are real or made-up. Making the transition from reading narrative texts to informational texts can be challenging for many students. The simple-to-follow format of narrative stories is one of the most common patterns that students know well. The narrative story pattern typically comes in one consistent format. On the other hand, the patterns that make up expository information can take a variety of formats. When information is packed in a storytelling format, learners comprehend and retain more of the information (Haven & Ducey, 2007).

> ### Common Core State Standards
>
> Grade 4: Report on a topic or text, tell a story, or recount an experience in an organized manner, using appropriate facts and relevant, descriptive details to support main ideas or themes; speak clearly at an understandable pace.

What the Informational Storytelling Intervention Looks Like

Everyone loves to hear a good story, but telling a good story can be just as fun. While we often think of stories as creative narratives, stories can also be informational. For example, history is a story that conveys important information about our past. Engaging in informational storytelling can help students prepare for informative writing, which will be covered in the next chapter. This type of information is organized in time sequence and imparts facts or information about a subject. The life-cycle of plants in science or individuals on a journey in history has a natural chronology that lends itself to informational storytelling (Grant & Littlejohn, 2005). Figure 5.1 shows the five basic parts of standard informational storytelling:

Figure 5.1   Informational Event

1. Topic and Context 2. Purpose 3. Events or Processes 4. Interpretations 5. Final Outcome
Topic and Context Who or What = Topic Where = Context Location When = Context Time
Purpose Challenge = Learn about content
Events or Processes 1. **Chronological Format:** First chronological event, second event, third event, and so forth. 2. **Compare/Contrast Format:** First comparisons, and then contrasts 3. **Cause/Effect Format:** First effects, and then what caused the effects
Key Effects = Significance of why this is important
Summarize Results = The final results of summary of the information

How the Informational Storytelling Intervention Works

1. **Invite students to look at a picture** in their textbook or one that you provide.

2. **Have students list 7–10 key vocabulary words** that describe the picture.

3. **Ask students to consider several questions** about the picture.

4. **Students should take the necessary time** to write down notes.

5. **Ask students to share the information** in a narrative storytelling with a partner.

6. **The teacher should ask students** to address informational storytelling by comparing/contrasting, showing cause/effect, using description/explanation, or providing sequential/time order.

7. **The partner should summarize the story** in their own words back to the informational story teller.

8. **Selected students can be asked to share** their stories in front of the entire class.

9. **Students should practice key speaking skills** that are outlined.

ELL Scaffolding

Work in a small group with the English Language Learners. Have students tell a story about a picture they are familiar with and value, like their family. As students share their story orally, make sure they include each of the five parts of the storytelling process.

Why the Informational Storytelling Intervention Works

As students become proficient in informational storytelling, they will be more comfortable reading to students in the early primary grades who benefit so much from interactions with older students. This speaking and listening process will strengthen students' ability to learn from pictures and develop their inferential creativity. Students who need help interpreting or understanding a picture will have a partner who can help them with key vocabulary and explanations. Students will become more familiar with the important processes of comparing and contrasting, chronological sequencing, describing, and noting causes and effects. Providing pictures for students serves as a scaffold for ELL students as they work on informational storytelling.

Progress Monitoring for the Informational Storytelling Intervention

Students can tell their own stories that they create from pictures that they draw. Ask students to consider several questions to jog their thinking. The following questions will help them make sure they have enough information to fill out and support their story.

♦ Who or what are the key components of the picture?

♦ What appears to be happening now?

♦ What do you think happened before to create this situation?

♦ What do you think will happen in the future?

♦ What differences are evident in the picture?

♦ What similarities are evident in the picture?

♦ What caused this situation, or what might be the effect of this situation?

♦ How can you describe the events that are occurring?

♦ What adjectives describe the people, events, or items in the picture?

♦ What do you know from history that could fill in parts of the story?

♦ Invite students to tell a descriptive, cause/effect, compare/contrast, or chronological sequence informational report of what is happening.

This strategy is engaging, and students will get better as they become involved and practice telling stories from a picture. Have students work in groups of two or three if they struggle to come up with ideas on their own.

Speaking Intervention #2: Structured Group Discussions

Students needed daily opportunities to discuss and share their thinking with peers. These opportunities to talk to classmates strengthen learning. When these discussions are more formally structured, students benefit both socially and academically. If students know the specific expectations of a structured discussion, they can focus more on the content of the conversation. Structured discussions build team dynamics in the classroom and support the development of small-group instruction. These skills are extremely important for students from low socioeconomic backgrounds who may not have these skills modeled at home (Daniel Levi, 2010). English Language Learners need a plethora of opportunities for engaging in classroom discourse. Many ELL students speak only their native language at home and in the community, so they need ample opportunities at school. Language development assessments highlight the need for ELLs to communicate in the following ways (CELDT):

♦ Ask for Information: "Excuse me, what is another word for happy?"

♦ Make a Request: "May I have a drink of water?"

♦ Offer Assistance: "Would you like me to help?"

♦ Ask for Clarification: "Did you say turn right in the hallway?"

♦ Give an Explanation: "Teachers ask questions to make us think."

Students often avoid engaging in group conversations because they do not know where to begin. The structured discourse skills help students understand the different purposes for engaging in conversations.

Structured Discourse Skills

♦ Expressing an Opinion

♦ Paraphrasing

♦ Asking for Clarification

♦ Soliciting a Response

♦ Acknowledging Other People's Ideas

♦ Offering a Suggestion

♦ Agreeing

♦ Disagreeing Politely

These discourse skills will go a long way to helping our students be effective communicators at school and beyond. Much of the discord and conflict at school can be attributed to ineffective communication. Students need to learn how to communicate at school in ways that will build teamwork and unity.

What the Structured Group Discussion Intervention Looks Like

This strategy clearly outlines for students how to engage in a high quality academic conversation. Structured group discussions can occur in groups of two or more. The structures of these group discussions will enhance the collaborative dynamics of the classroom. Killen (2006) emphasizes that structured discussions work extremely well in small cooperative groups and points out that "when students are not accustomed to learning through structured discussions you will need to explain to them how the discussion will be conducted . . . " (p. 154). Structured discussions begin with sentence frames that get students started on the right track. Many students avoid classroom conversations because they are unsure where to begin. Practicing the following sentence frames will help students build confidence and be more comfortable engaging in conversations with their peers (adapted from Johnson, 2009).

Structured Group Discussion Sentence Frames

Expressing an Opinion

- I believe that…
- It is my opinion that…

Paraphrasing

- In other words, you think…
- What I hear you saying is…

Soliciting a Response

♦ What do you think about...

♦ Do you agree with...

Acknowledging Other People's Ideas

♦ My idea is similar to _____'s idea that...

♦ I agree with _____ that...

Reporting a Group's Idea

♦ We agreed that...

♦ Our group believes that...

Offering a Suggestion

♦ Maybe we should consider...

♦ Here's something we might try...

Agreeing

♦ That's an interesting idea, I agree that...

♦ I hadn't thought of that; I like...

Disagreeing Politely

♦ Another idea is...

♦ I see it another way...

As students become proficient in dialoguing with these sentence frames, they will be able to communicate their purposes in class.

How the Structured Group Discussion Intervention Works

1. **Provide students with the various Structured Dialogue Sentence Frames** and explain their purposes.

2. **Model for students the various Structured Dialogue Sentence Frames** and demonstrate their benefits.

3. **Ask students to make a poster or make 3 × 5 cards** with the Structured Dialogue Sentence Frames on them for students to reference for content-area conversations.

4. **Place students in pairs** so that they can talk academically with each other about content-area material. (See Figure 5.2.)

5. **Provide each group with a topic** and ask them to practice discussing that topic.

Figure 5.2 A Structured Discussion in Action

6. **Provide students with the Structured Dialogue Sentence Frames** to elaborate on their ideas and academic talk (e.g , predicting, reflecting, clarifying).

7. **Once students have shared in pairs, they can meet with another pair of students** in a small group of four and exchange ideas.

8. **Several times a week, students should practice structured dialogue** until they can engage in each type of structured dialogue without the need for the sentence frames.

ELL Scaffolding

Ask students to work in pairs with ELL students as they practice structured discussions, so that ELLs can ask questions and receive peer support.

Why the Structured Group Discussion Intervention Works

Many students come to school without the conversational skills to work effectively with others, particularly their classroom peers. This strategy works because students need ample opportunities to negotiate language and interact with others. As students use the sentence frames, they will learn to share their individual ideas with peers. Students in general speak much more in small-group settings than in whole-class settings. They are also more comfortable in small-group settings. The sentence stems keep students on target and on topic. The responsibility of the listeners to respond to the speakers maintains the students' focus and keeps the conversations on track and productive.

Progress Monitoring for the Structured Group Discussion Intervention

As students are speaking to one another in pairs or in small groups of four, circulate throughout the classroom to listen to the quality of discussions that are taking place. Make sure to listen for students' level of content knowledge, use of vocabulary, and comfort level. As you listen intently to the various discussions shared by students, you will gain a lot of insights in a very short amount of time. After students share, take the time to reflect with students about the lessons they have learned about the content topic and about effective communication. As students practice using the various sentence stems and increase their comfort levels, remind them that the sentence stems should become internalized. Eventually students should be able to use the sentence stem starters without needing to refer to a poster on the wall or the 3 × 5 cards that list the sentence stems. Your students' confidence in speaking will increase as they internalize the sentence stems and can engage in a structured discussion naturally without the initial supports.

Speaking Intervention #3: Language Code-Switching

Code-Switching and Language Registers Academic Language is popping up as an issue for supporting English Language Learners, special education students, minority students, socioeconomically disadvantaged, and just about every other group of students who struggle (Wheeler & Swords, 2006). These struggling students often have difficulty with learning key terms and developing a depth and breadth of conceptual understanding. An example of an individual who code-switches effectively is Will Smith of *The Fresh Prince of Bel-Air* fame. Will Smith can rap and use the language of West Philadelphia where he was raised. Because he was raised by a school-teacher mom, he is also able to speak with an erudite vocabulary that is academic in nature. Will Smith won an Oscar for his supporting actor role in *Six Degrees of Separation*. The academy was amazed that Will could play the role of a prep school student adopted into a wealthy home. This role was a dramatic change from that in the television series *The Fresh Prince of Bel-Air* and the rapping career that gained him his initial fame.

Common Core State Standards

Grade 4: Differentiate between contexts that call for formal English (e.g., presenting ideas) and situations where informal discourse is appropriate (e.g., small-group discussion); use formal English when appropriate to task and situation.

What the Language Code-Switching Intervention Looks Like

Teachers seem to know intuitively that language is a key factor that separates many of the academic haves from the academic have-nots. Yet, many students feel that they may have only a very surface-level understanding of what academic language really means in practical terms. Code-switching helps students see the differences between casual conversations and academic conversations (Cantone, 2010). Students benefit from knowing different language registers and communicating using a variety of language registers to code-switch in their conversations (Isurin, Winford, & De Bot, 2009). Code-switching is the process of shifting between language registers or language styles to meet the purposes for communicating with a particular audience. For example, texting uses a different language register from presenting in front of a class. And, speaking to your friends in the neighborhood is a bit different than speaking to the Queen of England. Wolfram et al. (1999) point out that "linguistically rich classrooms provide many opportunities for children to talk on academic topics. To make this possible, social interaction structures need to be varied" (p. 126). The first thing to understand when learning to effectively code-switch is to recognize different types of language registers. Language registers have unique terminology and vernacular that separates them from other language registers. While there are hundreds of language registers, many of them can effectively be grouped into three types of language registers: casual, academic, and professional (Figure 5.3).

Figure 5.3 Code-Switching Language Registers

Type of Language Registers	Activities	Examples
Casual Language Register	Hobbies, Social Activities, Sports	Cooking, Football, Knitting, Scuba Diving
Academic Language Register	School, Formal Writing, Assessments, Curriculum	Textbooks, State Standards
Professional Language Register	Careers, Occupations	Policeman, Teacher, Auto Mechanic

Figure 5.4 provides some examples of casual language registers with which young students may be familiar.

The following examples of academic language registers (Figure 5.5) may take a little bit of time and effort to learn.

Students will need to learn professional language registers (Figure 5.6) if they desire to one day enter a particular profession.

It should be noted that casual language registers help students learn academic language registers, and academic language registers help students learn professional language registers.

How the Language Code-Switching Intervention Works

1. **Provide examples of key vocabulary** from different casual, academic, and professional language registers.

Figure 5.4 Casual Language Registers

Social Activity	Key Vocabulary
Street Talk	hood, benjamins, homies, bling-bling, check you out, got at ya, mack daddy, muggin, peeps
Texting	LOL, smiley face, aight, BFF, BTD, c ya, CUZ, def, FYF, grrlz, sry
Volleyball	spike, joust, bump, libero, setter, ace, pancake, block, jump serve, back row attack, double quick

Figure 5.5 Academic Language Registers

Academic Area	Key Vocabulary
Geography	latitude, cartography, prime meridian, isthmus, hemisphere, tundra, peninsula, continent
Assessment	summative, identify, diagnostic, formative, determine, most appropriate, benchmark, definition
Chemistry	elements, ions, acidic solution, hydrocarbon, ionic bond, gas, molecule, solvent, polymer, osmosis, mass

Figure 5.6 Professional Language Registers

Profession	Key Vocabulary
Police Officer	beat, APB, hit and run, ETA, breathalyzer, 10-4, suspect, custody, shift, 911
Teacher	schema, IEP, scaffolding, RTI, zone of proximal development, ELL, formative assessment
Auto Mechanic	transmission, spark plug, ignition, piston, cam shaft, O Rings, radiator, battery cables

2. **Ask students to share their own examples** of casual, academic, and professional language terms.

3. **Place students in groups of four** and ask them to share additional examples of various language registers.

4. **Provide groups with a variety of scripts** and ask them to identify the type of language register and key vocabulary.

5. **Invite students to code-switch** the language register of the script into another language register (e.g., academic to casual, casual to professional, Shakespeare to street language).

6. **Once students have altered scripts into a different language register,** have them present their scripts to the class by speaking and acting out the various parts.

7. **Ask students to share with the whole class** what they have learned about language registers and adjusting language to various social settings.

8. **Invite students to practice code-switching** their conversations in different situations.

ELL Scaffolding

ELLs can be asked to write in their own language a very casually-communicated paragraph, and next to it, a formal paragraph. Most languages have a casual and formal way of communicating. The teacher can then work with the students to translate the paragraphs into English.

Why the Language Code-Switching Intervention Works

This strategy works because it helps kids recognize that different settings and conversations require a different language register. Students will take greater ownership for the speaking and acting parts because they have been an integral part of the code-switching process. Providing students with a script establishes a starting as well as a scaffold that gives them direction as they progress. When students identify language registers and learn to code-switch to a different register, they understand more about how the language registers should be adjusted for various social settings. Asking students to share the language of texting or other casual language registers (e.g., horses, football, video games) puts them in the position of expert and places you the teacher in the role of learner. This switch of positions is empowering to students as they realize that various language registers are valuable. This strategy is a type of oral code-switching. For sixth-grade students, a teacher may introduce a passage from Shakespeare's "Romeo and Juliet," and then ask students to translate various dialogue passages into everyday English.

Progress Monitoring for the Language Code-Switching Intervention

Listen to students' use of vocabulary in the academic setting and to determine how well students use the academic language terms. Also, listen to students on the playground or at lunchtime to hear examples of the different language patterns they use in these casual settings. Have students make lists of academic language words and casual language words and compare them. You can watch examples of actors like Will Smith speaking very formally and then casually. See if students can then code-switch their language.

Speaking Intervention #4: Jigsaw Conversations

Students love to be part of the learning puzzle in class. The jigsaw intervention provides students with the opportunity first to learn and then to teach the information they have gleaned with their peers. Jigsaw conversations help students work in groups and it builds their reciprocal teaching abilities (Kruse, 2009). In this strategy, students become the expert in a topic, and they share or teach it to a small group of their classmates. Students can read resource material or listen to a video of an expert and then summarize what they learned for their group.

> ### Common Core State Standards
>
> Grade 5: Summarize a written text read aloud or information presented in diverse media and formats, including visually, quantitatively, and orally.
>
> Grade 5: Summarize the points a speaker makes and explain how each claim is supported by reasons and evidence.

What the Jigsaw Conversations Intervention Looks Like

This strategy allows students to work in "home" groups, where they will speak to their peers. Students will also work in "expert" groups, where they will study specific information. After working with their "expert" peers, they will reconvene with their "home" groups to teach them all that they have learned. Jigsaw conversations are one more way to organize students into groups where they are proactive participants at the center of learning. Because students are very motivated to share their expertise, they often are less conscious of the responsibility to speak in front of their peers and communicate effectively.

How the Jigsaw Conversations Intervention Works

1. **Place four to five students in each jigsaw "home" group.** The groups should be diverse in terms of gender, cultural background, and ability.

2. **Divide the day's lesson into four to five parts.** For example, if you want students to learn about Martin Luther King, Jr., ask different students to talk about (1) marches, (2) speeches, (3) growing up, (4) family life, and (5) beliefs.

3. **Assign study topics for each student to learn his or her part,** making sure students have the necessary resources.

4. **Give students time to read over their parts** and become familiar with the information.

5. **Have students move to temporary "expert" groups** by having one student from each jigsaw group join with other students assigned the same part. Provide students time to discuss the main ideas and rehearse their speaking presentations that they will share with their jigsaw group.

6. **Have students return to their "home" jigsaw groups,** after they have prepared their presentations.

7. **Invite students to share their parts with their "home" groups** while the rest of the group listens and asks clarifying questions.

8. **Students can give a quick three-question quiz to the other members** of their jigsaw group at the end of all the presentations.

9. **Reconvene as a class and review key concepts** that you want students to remember.

ELL Scaffolding

English Language Learners enjoy working in the comfort of small groups. They can practice their speaking skills on their peers. As a positive climate is established in the classroom, students will help ELLs and others who need help.

Why the Jigsaw Conversations Intervention Works

Students enjoy being experts on a particular subject. The jigsaw strategy gives students the chance to learn and share their knowledge with a group of peers. Students like to be in the role of teacher, especially when they are in the comfort of a small group. This speaking and teaching opportunity will enhance their confidence, as all of the speaking strategies do. This strategy works because students are less conscious of their speaking responsibilities and instead are focused on conveying the content they have learned. The comfort of the small group enhances learning as each student has an equal opportunity to speak and listen. While many students will avoid engaging with adults, they will, on the other hand, prepare and perform for their peers.

Progress Monitoring for the Jigsaw Conversations Intervention

This strategy provides ample opportunities to rotate around the room and to listen to how students are doing. If students struggle to master the content required to play the role of expert, provide ideas and support. You can also have groups evaluate how well each member of the group is performing, and how the group collectively spoke about the topics provided. Use a simple rubric for students to give feedback. This is a very student-centered activity that allows teachers to rotate through groups, listening and providing support as needed. Students within the expert groups can help ELLs prepare the content of their presentations.

Speaking Intervention #5:
Academic Content Talk

It is important for students to talk intelligently about a variety of academic content areas. We expect our students to communicate about content areas, such as social studies, science, math, language arts. English Language Learners and special-needs students may lack confidence in talking about academic topics. When students engage frequently in academic talk with their peers and adults, their level of content understanding increases significantly (Neuman & Dickinson, 2010). This intervention strategy looks very similar to Speaking Intervention #2: Structured Group Discussions, yet it differs in its purposes. While structured discussions are designed to help students engage effectively in any conversation, academic talk is explicitly designed to expand content knowledge. The following skills help students talk in ways that extend their understanding of academic content:

- ◆ Tapping Prior Knowledge
- ◆ Predicting
- ◆ Picturing
- ◆ Internal Questioning
- ◆ Making Connections
- ◆ Generalizing
- ◆ Forming Interpretations
- ◆ Clarifying Issues

- Relating Our Learning

- Summarizing

- Reflecting on Our Learning

As students talk with their peers and negotiate processes like summarizing, reflecting, and generalizing, they will increase their understanding of the academic content being discussed.

Common Core State Standards

Grade 6: Engage effectively in a range of collaborative discussions (one-on-one, in groups, and teacher-led) with diverse partners on grade 6 topics, texts, and issues, building on others' ideas and expressing their own clearly.

- Come to discussions prepared, having read or studied required material; explicitly draw on that preparation by referring to evidence on the topic, text, or issue to probe and reflect on ideas under discussion.

- Follow rules for collegial discussions, set specific goals and deadlines, and define individual roles as needed.

What the Academic Content Talk Intervention Looks Like

Academic content talk is a critical part of creating quality conversations in the classroom. Every content-area course, whether it is social studies, science, science, or mathematics, benefits from focused dialogue that engages students in the rich content of each subject. Students need plenty of opportunities to engage in conversations that focus on academic content. Fisher, Rothenberg, & Frey (2008) note that "when teachers plan for talk and clearly establish the purpose and expectations, students use academic language and vocabulary in authentic ways" (p. 42). The following sentence frames help students enter into academic conversations and stay focused on the content of the lesson (adapted from Johnson, 2009).

Academic Talk Sentence Frames

Tapping Prior Knowledge

- I already know that…
- This reminds me of…
- This relates to…

Predicting

- I guess that…
- I believe that…
- I hypothesize that…

Picturing

- I can see…
- I can imagine…
- I can picture in my mind…

Clarifying Issues

- I have a question about…
- I'm unsure about…
- How did _____ happen…

Making Connections

- This is like…
- This reminds me of…
- This is connected to…

Asking Questions of Others

- I wonder why…
- What if…
- Why does…

Forming Interpretations

- What this means to me is…
- The idea I'm getting is…
- I think this represents…

Reflecting on Learning

- The most important idea I learned today was…
- The most challenging part of our learning was…
- My favorite idea was…

As students get familiar with these sentence frames, they will increase their comfort level with academic conversations in the classroom.

How the Academic Content Talk Intervention Works

1. **Give students the various Academic Talk Sentence Frames** and explain their purposes.

2. **Model for the class** the various Academic Talk Sentence Frames.

3. **Ask students to make a poster or 3 × 5 cards** listing the Academic Talk Sentence Frames for students to reference for content-area conversations.

4. **Place students in groups of four** so that they can talk academically with each other about content-area conversations.

5. **Provide each group with a content-area passage** and ask them to read the passage out loud together as a group.

6. **Ask students to identify the main idea,** or gist, of the topic.

7. **Have students use the Academic Talk Sentence Frames** to elaborate on their ideas and engage in academic talk (e.g , predicting, reflecting, clarifying) to reinforce their learning.

8. **Several times a week, students should practice academic talk** until they can engage in each type of structured dialogue without the need for the sentence frames.

Figure 5.7 shows an academic talk discussion in action.

Figure 5.7 Academic Talk

Why the Academic Content Talk Intervention Works

Academic content talk helps students get started with a focused content discussion with a peer. The sentence frames for this strategy provide scaffolded support that helps students feel comfortable engaging in content conversations. Students (especially ELLs) like knowing that they are off to the right start and can inject their own language and ideas to complete the sentence frames. Students benefit from frequent practice engaging in academic content talk. Their ability to stay focused on the topic, on listening to a peer, and on processing the information increases significantly. This strategy keeps students on track and makes peer-to-peer dialogues in class much more successful. Without academic talk, pair-share activities often get off-track, and students spend their time talking about social issues rather than academic content. The quality of student thinking and the quality of content-area conversations will improve dramatically in the classroom.

Progress Monitoring for the Academic Content Talk Intervention

After assigning the sentence frames and discussion topic, the teacher should move from group to group and listen carefully to the manner in which the students communicate about the content topic. Students who are being brief in their comments should be asked to clarify, expand, and so forth from Intervention Strategy #1 listed on page 116. Listen to students to make sure they use academic language. You will notice that the Academic Talk Sentence Frames will keep students on topic as they discuss in-depth the content-area ideas. You will see the richness of classroom conversations increase. Students will become more comfortable thinking more broadly and more deeply as they frame their thinking and communicate it to their classmates. Work with struggling students one-on-one so you can see their progress before letting them work with their peers. Students are excited to share their thinking and ideas with their peers, so this gives them incentive to learn the skills quickly.

Summing It Up

Students who master the art of speaking become more confident learners and leaders. As we provide frequent speaking opportunities in our classrooms, our students will increase their capacity to improve their own learning as well as that of their peers. Informational storytelling provides students with a comfortable format for sharing stories with their peers. Code-switching helps students recognize the different language registers that people use in different social settings. As students develop the ability to code-switch, they will become better communicators. Structured group discussions provide the sentence frames that build students' confidence. Through this strategy, students also become better listeners. Jigsaw conversations allow students to be the expert and share new knowledge with their classmates. Academic talk strengthens students' thinking and enhances their ability to engage in content conversations. Language production may be the most important area for improving English Language Learners' ability to communicate effectively. All students will benefit from speaking in the comfort of the classroom among their peers.

Reflection

1. How well do your students engage in structured discussions and academic talk in class?
2. Do your students have opportunities to speak in class every day about content topics?

6

Grades 3–6 Writing Intervention Strategies

*"Writing is an act of faith,
not a trick of grammar."*

—E. B. White

Katie lacks structure in her life at school and at home. Her backpack is a messy, overflowing satchel of smudged and wrinkled papers stuffed together. The contents spill out every time she opens it. Like her backpack, Katie is full of good ideas, but her thinking is often imprecise and all over the place. She has lots of wonderful perspectives, and she likes to share them with others. Yet every time she tries, they bubble out in a random fashion. She does not know what to do with feedback from others and typically tosses her graded papers in her backpack or in the garbage the first chance she gets. Even her creative writing seems to just spin on and on without really ever arriving anywhere. Her stories never finish. They just conclude at some undetermined point. It seems that with all of her great starts, Katie struggles to finish things. Katie is a random writer.

Writing in Grades 3–6

After receiving feedback about his story, a student commented that writing is making your "words stick." He explained that when you are speaking, there is no accountability for the language you use, but in writing the words are "stuck" on paper. People can read your thoughts, even see thoughts, and if you are good with words, the reader can jump into your story or learn from you. But the best part of writing is that you can go back and read the words again. They are stuck on the page exactly as you wrote them. He decided then that reading makes you smart but writing makes you smarter. Without knowing it, he aptly described why writing is so important to literacy and to successful college and career readiness. Whether it be an opinion, argument, exposé, factual summary, real or imagined story, or a sensory description, the ability to capture thoughts and communicate them through written expression is the fundamental skill set for all academic and career pursuits. Making words "stick" so that they are retrievable and cause others to think, know, and feel is the purpose for teaching writing.

Writing for young students builds upon the skills developed in the strategies discussed in Chapters 2–5: listening, reading, computing, and speaking. While students in grades 3–6 can come to school without the robust listening and language skills needed to succeed, if writing skills are taught effectively students can usually stay on track. So, laying the proper groundwork for writing and providing effective instruction in writing is important for all students. Because writing is a high-level literacy skill, it involves much negotiation of meaning between the student-author and a selected audience. In a similar fashion, reading involves a negotiation of meaning between the reader-audience and the author. Successful young students start to develop an internally negotiated dialogue with the author when reading, and they develop an internally negotiated dialogue with the audience when writing (Donohue, 2007). It is truly an important day in the life of a young student when he or she consistently identifies and engages with the author as a negotiating reader-audience or with the audience as a negotiating writer-author. In many ways, writing is the culminating activity for language and literacy. It is the skill or domain that showcases students' ability to organize their thoughts into learning. Conveying ideas in an organized fashion to an audience is a skill that will pay dividends for our students for many years to come. While our students need to continue to listen, read, compute, and speak effectively to prepare for college or their career, writing is most likely the primary method for showcasing and evaluating their ability and talents. So, this chapter will look at several intervention and instructional approaches that help keep students at grade level and prepare them for their current writing challenges as well as those in their future.

Effective Writing

The literature on career and college readiness indicates that writing is the most remediated skill in the first two years of college and the most problematic for employers (Stanley, 2009). Writing effectively is vital to future success. When we start the process of teaching writing with students and ask them what they think it is or how it might best be defined, they invariably define writing in terms of the subskills that are required to do it well. They call out, "Writing is sentences with periods" or "Writing is about putting words on paper." Some say that writing is about knowing rules. More sophisticated students guess that writing is linked to a purpose. For example, writing tells a story or describes something; perhaps it is someone's argument that persuades you to change your opinion or educates you. In these guesses, the students have tapped into what good writing does for a reader. They have started to define four of the basic benefits of reading and the effects of effective writing. Most readers enjoy

1. a good story that follows a consistent pattern,
2. vivid descriptions that create pictures in their minds,
3. learning specific facts from what they read, and
4. finding out what other people think and feel.

Writing is a capstone learning activity that requires students to have a robust understanding of language and literacy. Like Katie at the beginning of this chapter, students need consistent opportunities to organize and synthesize their thinking through writing. This time and effort will pay off in helping Katie—and students like her—become more organized in her thinking, even though her backpack may never be sorted out. Informal, daily quick-writes can help Katie learn to write with some level of genre automaticity. As with speaking, feedback is a key factor in writing improvement and competence. The use of peer editing and revision is often the most potent form of feedback; it accomplishes two objectives: it creates opportunities for productive use of academic language, and it makes the transition from oral form to print form a reality.

Speaking or talking prepares students for eventually conveying their ideas in written form. Figure 6.1 (page 140) shows how writing floats on top of a sea of language.

Ultimately, effective writing reveals our thinking and demonstrates our ideas.

Figure 6.1 The Ship of Writing Success

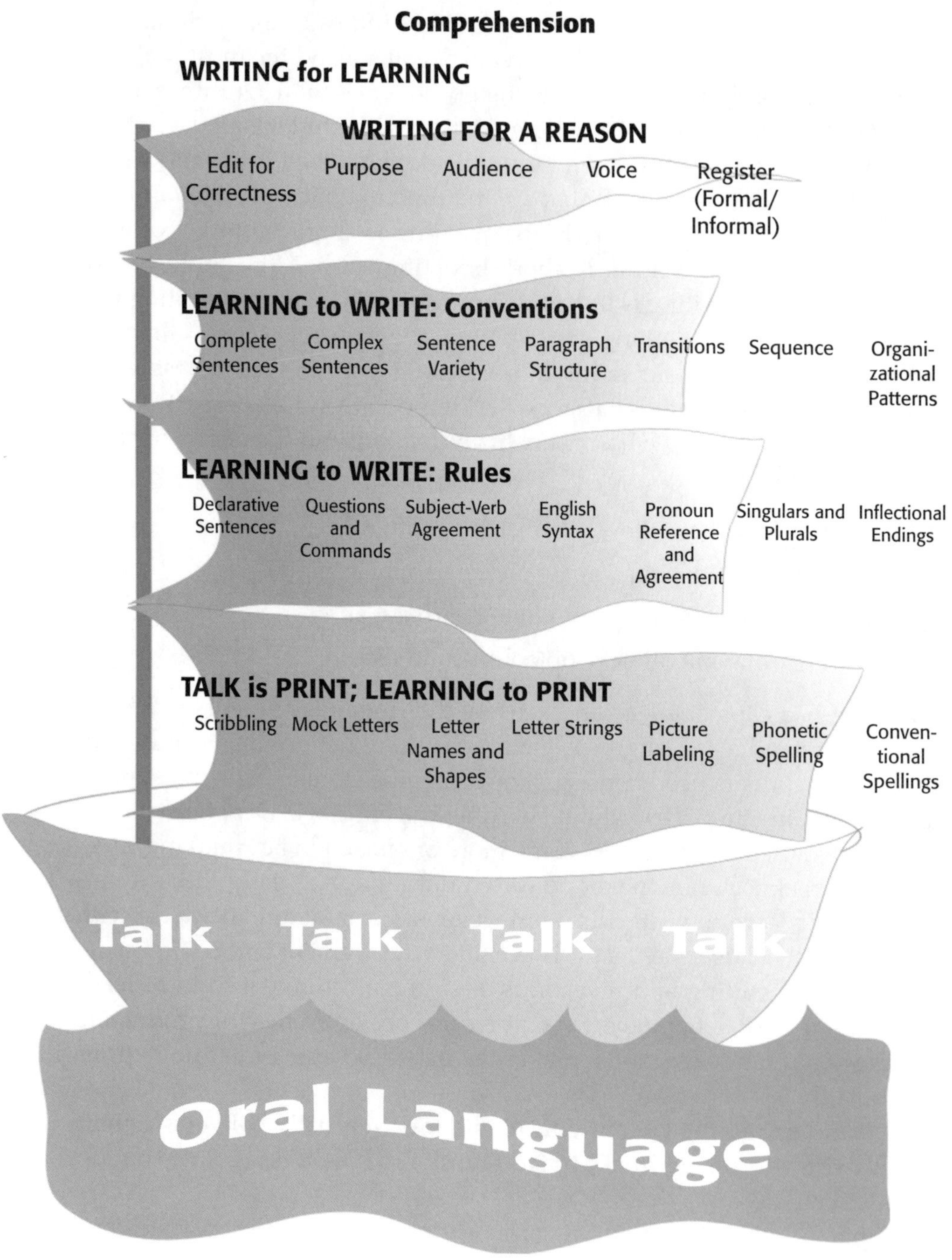

Comprehension

WRITING for LEARNING

WRITING FOR A REASON

Edit for Correctness | Purpose | Audience | Voice | Register (Formal/Informal)

LEARNING to WRITE: Conventions

Complete Sentences | Complex Sentences | Sentence Variety | Paragraph Structure | Transitions | Sequence | Organizational Patterns

LEARNING to WRITE: Rules

Declarative Sentences | Questions and Commands | Subject-Verb Agreement | English Syntax | Pronoun Reference and Agreement | Singulars and Plurals | Inflectional Endings

TALK is PRINT; LEARNING to PRINT

Scribbling | Mock Letters | Letter Names and Shapes | Letter Strings | Picture Labeling | Phonetic Spelling | Conventional Spellings

Talk   Talk   Talk   Talk

Oral Language

Publishing Writing

The reasons people read can be easily translated into different types of writing. Different types of writing parallel the different reasons people like to read. People like to read stories (Narrative Writing), gather new information and knowledge (Informative Writing) and be convinced or validated about an opinion, bias, or belief (Opinion-Based Writing or Argument) (Kendall Haven, 2004). Students should spend time with their words, thoughts, and reflections to produce a publishable example of their work. We have a generous view of what *publishable* means—from our educational perspective, a publishable work meets the established rubric, benchmarks, or standards of record, and "being published" requires only that the work be displayed or presented for review. Libraries provide venues for publishing as do hallways, cafeterias, and dedicated classroom areas. We recommend that hallways serve for postings of all original texts in all genres at all grade levels. It is always a good practice to "publish," or post, student work next to a picture of the student because this increases the feedback students receive informally from peers, other teachers, and other adults on campus. Success breeds success; so it is with writing. An author with positive reviews tends to want to write more and more often. Pasting the halls with homegrown literature begets more publishing from the classroom. Sixth graders can use the third-grade standards to write a narrative (story) with a plot and characters appropriate to third graders, and the third graders can write a descriptive critique of the sixth-grade authors. "Post offices" work in elementary schools, especially if there is a "postmaster general" who passes out themes for the week or the month. Recipients of quality mail can submit their correspondence for school publication in the cafeteria. The postmaster can choose those selections that get published. The key to these practices is the expectation of excellence that is framed by explicit criteria in the form of a rubric or through the use of the standards. Writing allows our students to showcase their language, literacy, and learning.

Good Writers Are Good Thinkers

Writing is a means for developing and clarifying students thinking—good writers are good thinkers. Because every student has good ideas and can think well, every student can in time become a good writer. As our friend Brad Wilcox says, "If you can think it, you can write it." Writing is a balance between creative, tangential ideas and structured, orderly construction of those ideas. Writing develops the best thinking within students (Romano, 1987).

Teachers can have students write to discover, create and explore their thinking, dig up prior knowledge, to cultivate intellectual independence, to conjecture about possibilities, to struggle with difficult concepts, and to engage the imagination as an ally in learning. (p. 43)

For example, a quick-write might be to write an informational paragraph with a literacy buddy summarizing the content of this chapter. This allows the student dyad to talk about the content, craft thoughts from oral expression to written text, and receive feedback from a peer regarding perception similarities and differences. These quick-writes can happen as a means to close a lesson, front-load, check for background knowledge, or provide a venue to transition from various core subject areas. Formal writing can be practiced daily to check for understanding throughout the delivery of core curriculum and needs to occur at least several times a week for student thinking to develop effectively. Research shows that the average fourth-grade classroom engages students in 90 minutes of writing a week (only 31 percent of the time), while classrooms with successful interventions and superior results do so 83 percent of the time (Nagin, 2003). Providing consistent writing opportunities will produce greater academic results for students.

Writing is a personally creative activity where students use words to produce original text. To be a writer, students must pull together their thoughts, organize them, and put them into words using language conventions. Student writers, then, have to be thinkers and organizers capable of following consistent formats for conveying their thoughts. Students add to this equation their own creative thoughts and individual ideas that make their writing unique and personal. Every student has the capacity to be an author: a confident, capable writer. Writing is the ultimate creative act. Students' discovery of how they can be creative with their writing is what makes all of this so worthwhile. It is also a great mirror for future careers and expertise. Learning to be an effective writer can change the direction of a student's life.

Writing Intervention #1: Writing Aloud

Children make predictions about how written language works and create stories based on these best guesses or predictions. The best interactive stories written with children often are the result of endings based on their ideas or pictures of how things should have worked in a narrative. Writing aloud is a terrific language experience approach strategy that helps grades 3–6 writers master the variety of elements involved in writing. When Professor Roach Van Allen first described this approach, he showed how it creates a most natural bridge between spoken language and written language:

- What I can think about, I can talk about.

- What I can say, I can write.

- What I can write, I can read.

- I can read what I can write and what other people can write for me to read.

Writing aloud provides us as teachers the opportunity to model and talk explicitly about the important processes involved in writing for our students. Through write-alouds, we outline and help organize the larger ideas while at the same time divulging the subtle nuances that make up a writer's thinking and decisions. Writing aloud also works well with shared writing (Johnson & Karns, 2011) because they are both collaborative processes that involve everyone in the class. Writing aloud should be modeled and demonstrated to students at least once a week during the school year. Teacher demonstrations of the writing process through write-alouds are a critical element in a successful writer's workshop (Cunningham & Allington, 1999).

Common Core State Standards

Grade 3: With guidance and support from adults, produce writing in which the development and organization are appropriate to task and purpose. (Grade-specific expectations for writing types are defined in standards 1–3.)

Grade 3: With guidance and support from peers and adults, develop and strengthen writing as needed by planning, revising, and editing.

What the Writing Aloud Intervention Looks Like

Writing aloud makes explicit all of the important thinking that goes on in a good/expert writer's head. Writing aloud can be a bit messy, with plenty of corrections and revisions to demonstrate that getting one's thinking down in an effective fashion takes time and consideration. Write-alouds should be scaffolded and explained in terms that the slowest or lowest learner in the class can grasp and understand. Write-alouds can model any variety of types, styles, or genres of writing (e.g., persuasive, informative, narrative, poetry, paragraphs, essays). When revealing our thinking as writers, we should use a tone that guides or suggests. For example, it is better to say, "I wonder if we should use a different example here. How might we do that?" rather than "This definitely needs a different example." When writing aloud, making an occasional "accidental" writing error can help students pay attention to see where they can correct and improve errors in the writing. Making accidental errors also shows that writing does not need to come out perfectly. Some write-alouds should be completed during the lesson, while other write-alouds, like two-page essays, may take several days to complete. In this way students will see that different writing projects can be extended or ongoing.

How the Writing Aloud Intervention Works

Before Write-Alouds

1. **Select a writing assignment that is appropriate for your students** and determine the scope of the assignment. (e.g., Writing persuasively for one paragraph focused on constructing good topic sentences)

2. **Make sure students know the writing genre** (e.g., poetry, paragraph, short story) that will be addressed, and show students a model or example of this on the overhead projector/document camera.

3. **Have students identify the audience** that their writing will be directed towards. (e.g., the city mayor, classmates, experts, family)

4. **Collectively choose a topic** and discuss a title to write about. (e.g., Abraham Lincoln, whales, freedom)

5. **Ask students to think-pair-share** about ideas, background experiences, reasons, or examples that may support the chosen topic. (e.g., zoo, Sea World, orcas, humpbacks)

6. **Have students fill out a graphic organizer** or organize some of the thinking and ideas that come from students in the class. (e.g., story map, outline, fact, opinion, description)

During Write-Alouds

1. **Ask lots of questions out loud as you begin constructing your writing.** You can go through a model paper and review all of the questions the writer may have asked as the writing was constructed.

2. **Model asking questions out loud** as you consider the different aspects of the writing assignment, like "What is the topic I want to write about?" or "How can I grab the audience's attention?"

3. **Write and say out loud the processes going through your head** as you determine the introductory sentence for the topic and, with the class's help, re-work the sentence after your initial effort in order to provide an attention-grabber.

4. **Construct supporting sentences** and select examples, reasons, quotes, or supporting details that reinforce the topic sentences.

5. **Through writing aloud you can review basic writing principles,** such as conventions, word choice, sentence structure, paragraph transitions, and figurative language, as you write in front of the class on the overhead or whiteboard.

6. **Make sure to show students how to negotiate the writing challenges** they will face in class assignments. For example, about writing format you can say, "How should my first sentence begin?" About word choice, "I like the word *informs* better than *explains* here." About sentence structure, "Let's make these two sentences into one compound sentence."

7. **Students can provide examples from their own current writing challenges** for you to model potential solutions and provide support. Students enjoy seeing their teacher improve their writing.

After Write-Alouds

1. **Ask students to go back and see if sentences can be combined** or if better transitions or word choice can be used to enhance meaning.

2. **Invite students to evaluate their writing** based on clear standards or a rubric.

3. **Invite students to enhance or edit their classmates' writing** to help make it even better.

4. **Have students record in a writing journal** their thoughts about the writing and what they learned.

ELL Scaffolding

Spend time writing aloud in small groups with ELL students to review the writing process lessons in a more intimate setting where these students can receive additional attention. ELLs will be able to ask more questions and receive more explicit input and feedback. Be extra encouraging and provide more time since ELL students often think in their native language and then translate into English before they can write their thinking down on paper.

---

5. **Remember you can use write-alouds before any writing assignment** to provide model examples and discuss the key thinking and processes that go into good writing.

Why the Writing Aloud Intervention Works

Students always benefit from seeing a model of what great writing should look like. It is best if the writing shown to students is from students in previous classes who have demonstrated successful grade-level writing. The teacher's write-aloud process scaffolds the type of thinking that effective writers follow, and it shows them what to do. Good writers are good thinkers. And writing aloud makes this much more evident to students. Using relevant writing challenges from students' current work as examples for improving writing or overcoming writing blocks is very engaging for students. They like to see their writing go through the process of improvement, and they like to see the writing examples and challenges their peers also face. Writing aloud provides a sense of safety and security to young writers who still may be finding their voice and confidence. This intervention works because it is sequential and scaffolds the core content of how to write into simple deliverables that are modeled for students. When write-alouds are conducted on a weekly basis and discrete skills (e.g., punctuation, topic sentences) are addressed, student writing will consistently improve. This strategy works because it provides safe, scaffolded support that helps students first visualize and then construct writing that is modeled after effective processes.

Progress Monitoring for the Writing Aloud Intervention

Ask students to write on whiteboards to show their involvement and to get them to think along with the teacher. Students can write down their best thinking for a sentence or word choice, and then the teacher can select the sentence or word choice that will be recorded.

♦ Frame thinking in the form of questions that the students will help answer. For example, "What type of punctuation does this sentence need?" or "What would be a good transition word to start this sentence?"

♦ After modeling a write-aloud, students should be asked to construct their own similar sentences or paragraphs to show that they are grasping the processes that were modeled.

♦ Check the sentences and paragraphs to make sure that students are mastering the skills covered.

Once skills are developed for older students (grades 5–6), selected students can lead write-alouds for the class at the overhead projector as long as they have been thoroughly prepared and the write-aloud is well scripted ahead of time.

Writing Intervention #2: Paragraph-Style Writing

This writing intervention provides an engaging process for students to scaffold both their creative and their researched ideas into standard paragraph structure. Students need to learn to support what they think and why (opinion); tell stories that are both personal and nonfictional (narrative); and they must know how to tell what they know (informative/explanatory). These writing styles—opinion, narrative, and informative/explanatory—are identified well by the experts who authored the Common Core State Standards for students in grades 3–6. They make it clear that each style requires a unique set of skills and provides the student with additional information on how best to communicate thoughts, ideas, feelings, and knowledge.

Common Core Paragraph-Style Genres

- **Opinion:** viewpoint, contrast, and reasons

- **Narrative**: beginning, middle, and end

- **Informative**: topic, support, and summary

By third grade, students respond differently to various genres or writing methods (Langer, 1985). Paragraph-style writing works best for opinion-based and informative writing, yet the skills developed in this strategy can also assist narrative writing. Any writing activity that requires students to follow a paragraph-style format (e.g., journals, reports) will benefit from this intervention.

Common Core State Standards

Grade 4: Write routinely over extended time frames (time for research, reflection, and revision) and shorter time frames (a single sitting or a day or two) for a range of discipline-specific tasks, purposes, and audiences.

What the Paragraph-Style Writing Intervention Looks Like

Writing interventions need to engage in easily sequenced steps that can be repeated until observations and assessments indicate that the student understands how to do the lesson with some level of automaticity. Interventions strive to bring up familiar core content in new ways so that the struggling students can see another way of doing or accomplishing the task, a way that they can better understand and absorb. Interventions should set the students up to be successful. Repeated success provides the motivation for attempting increasingly difficult tasks. Consider the following graphic organizer (Figure 6.2) for helping students organize their ideas.

Writing interventions need to engage in easily sequenced steps that can be repeated until observations and assessments indicate that the student understands how to do the lesson with some level of autonomy. Interventions strive to bring up familiar core content in new ways so that the struggling student can see another way of doing or accomplishing the task that he or she can better understand and absorb.

How the Paragraph-Style Writing Intervention Works

1. **Talk about different stages or levels for developing writing skills.** For example, students first learn about letters, then syllables, then words (eight parts of speech), then sentences (four types of sentences), then paragraphs (paragraph purposes, e.g., persuasive, informative),

Figure 6.2 Paragraph Writing Organizer

Topic Sentence: Killer whales are typically friendly animals that do not really deserve their violent name.
Supporting Sentence #1: These black-and-white whales are also known as Orcas. **Supporting Sentence #2:** Killer whales are friendly mammals who live in families or pods. **Supporting Sentence #3:** Killer whales live in the cool ocean waters of the Pacific Northwest in Puget Sound.
Concluding Sentence: Killer whales will swim next to boats and jump playfully out of the water as they play with their family.

then essays (five-paragraph essay), then chapters of a book, and finally a book.

2. **Share with the class that the structure of words** includes letters, syllables, sounds, and so forth.

3. **Share with the class that the structure of sentences** includes words, parts of speech, punctuation, subjects, predicates, phrases, clauses, and so forth.

4. **Share with the class that the structure of paragraphs** includes topic sentences, supporting sentences, concluding sentences, and so forth.

5. **Let the class know that you are going to discuss a standard five-sentence paragraph,** and ask the class to share what they think the five sentences may be that make up a basic paragraph.

6. **Introduce the idea of a topic sentence** and provide examples of good topic sentences that answer *who?* or *what?* is being discussed. Practice writing different topic sentences with the class.

7. **Introduce the idea of three supporting sentences** and provide examples of good supporting sentences that have lots of descriptive detail. Practice writing different supporting sentences with the class about a specific topic.

8. **Introduce the idea of a concluding sentence** and provide examples of good concluding sentences that summarize the significance of the topic. Practice writing different supporting sentences with the class.

9. **Have students construct a standard paragraph** with at least five sentences.

10. **Ask students to exchange and edit** classmates' paragraphs.

11. **Reflect with students about paragraph writing** and discuss what they have learned.

12. **Practice with students a variety of different paragraph writing assignments.**

ELL Scaffolding

Ask students to read what they have written out loud to check if it sounds right.

Why the Paragraph-Style Writing Intervention Works

The benefits of reading are translated easily into types of writing. The types of writing parallel why people read. They read stories (narrative), gather new information and knowledge (informative), and read to be convinced or validated about an opinion, bias, or belief (opinion-based). This intervention works because it is sequential and scaffolds the core content of how to write into simple deliverables. It is also valuable because it incorporates the use of a nonlinguistic representation through the graphic organizer. When graphic organizers are used well, they become the "thinking maps" that can become the basis of writing. They are the basis of outlines that students will write in the future for research and informative writing.

Progress Monitoring for the Paragraph-Style Writing Intervention

Check to see if students have a clear idea about the topic they want to write about. Some students need more background information to help them write successfully about their topic. Go to the library or browse the Internet to provide students with more information that supports their topic. One of the best ways to help students understand how to compose a paragraph is to do it with them interactively. Interactive planning and writing involves students in a practice that will generally foster success at the personal level. Successful writing requires that you know your subject. It is best either to use their personal experience or to give them information to write a fact-based demonstrative piece. The formula for formative assessments that will give you broad-based data about what the child knows and needs to know includes:

- Does your first sentence address your topic?

- Did you stay on the same topic throughout the paragraph?

- Did you provide the reader with supporting details about the topic?

- Does the last sentence summarize the significance of the topic?

Beyond the above checks linked to content and grade-level standards, these evaluative questions can be used to help student review their use of the written genres: Did the format of the expression communicate effectively the message that was intended? Can you list three to five points that you were trying to convey? Can you summarize the key points from the written presentation? What are they? Do they align? Why or why not? Remind the student that writing is the skill of crafting text to send messages that are received as intended.

Writing Intervention #3:
Opinion-Based Writing

The Common Core State Standards make it clear that students need to learn several different types of writing to best communicate their thoughts, ideas, feelings, and knowledge. From these, the more specific writing techniques can be grown and honed.

♦ Opinion-based writing (called argument in the upper grades) is structured and reason based.

♦ Narrative writing is structured and story based.

♦ Informative writing is research and fact based.

The three genres—narrative, informative, and opinion—are vitally important for young students to learn so that they can more fully develop their cognitive ability. Students need to learn to support what they think and why (opinion); tell stories that are both personal and nonfictional (narrative); and they must know how to tell what they know and check for validity (informative). Learning to write within the constructs of a specific genre is organized much like a ladder. Each genre requires an understanding of all of the successive steps to get to a successful result at the end. The ladder works backwards. These ladder steps are listed on the next page and can be used to provide organization to paragraph-style writing or to write-aloud strategies. The steps begin at the bottom of the ladder and progress to the top.

While all three types of writing have commonalities (e.g., description, answering questions for the audience, paragraph structure), opinion-based or argument writing leans on the difference between factual statements and opinion statements, as shown in Figure 6.3 (page 152).

What the Opinion-Based Writing Intervention Looks Like

Opinion-based writing gets the audience involved. It is compelling and speaks to the reader as either a majority opinion (e.g., Students should have recess every day!) or a contrary idea (e.g., Only students that complete all of their homework should get to go to recess!). The issues addressed in opinion-based writing should be ones that will convince a specific audience or targeted group of readers. The writer must give enough facts and details to engage the reader and encourage the reader to take action. (e.g., If you believe as I do, sign this petition!) Finally, opinion and argumentative writing must include a summary or closing. (e.g., Dr. Phil agrees with us. He says that all middle school students should not start school until after 10:00 A.M. because

Figure 6.3 **Key Writing Genres in Grades 3–6**

Opinion	Informative	Narrative
Summarizes your winning thought	Closes with a summary of information or a final piece of advice	Tells the end of the story with your feelings
Provides specific facts	Uses a variety of resources to document presentation	Makes the tale real and tells it from a personal perspective
Uses references to validate an opinion	Provides explicit details and explanations	Uses extensive description and the five Ws: who, what, when, where, and why
Uses strong language to convince someone or share an opinion	Clearly outlines the information and where you got it	Explains why you are telling the story
States the argument	Explains the topic and why it was chosen	States the first event in the story
Opinion	Informative	Narrative

> **Common Core State Standards**
>
> Grade 6: Write arguments to support claims with clear reasons and relevant evidence.
>
> ◆ Introduce claim(s) and organize the reasons and evidence clearly.
>
> ◆ Support claim(s) with clear reasons and relevant evidence, using credible sources and demonstrating an understanding of the topic or text.
>
> ◆ Use words, phrases, and clauses to clarify the relationships among claim(s) and reasons.
>
> ◆ Establish and maintain a formal style.
>
> ◆ Provide a concluding statement or section that follows from the argument presented.

Figure 6.4   Distinguishing Fact from Opinion

Fact	Opinion
Music classes are no longer offered at my school.	Music classes are an important part of a good education.
Mount Rainier has a height of 14,441 feet.	Mount Rainier is my favorite mountain.
No Child Left Behind was passed by Congress in 2001.	No Child Left Behind places too much emphasis on testing.
The school cafeteria serves pizza every Friday.	The school cafeteria needs to serve food that is healthier.

they need more rest than at any other time in their development. So, if you really enjoy healthy living, sleep, sleep, sleep, and sign this petition to start school later than 7:00 A.M.). In the Common Core State Standards for Writing, one of the first challenges is to learn to present and support an opinion. Your students should be able to consider two statements and identify which one is a fact and which is an opinion. Facts state what happened; opinions share how someone feels or why he or she thinks a certain way. This opinion has to be verifiable and requires evidence to complete the task satisfactorily. Learning to state an opinion and validate it with concrete statements is the basis for all research and gives students access to the core curriculum. Make sure students can properly identify factual statements from statements of opinion (Figure 6.4).

Determining the difference between fact and opinion is a critical skill for young students (Clifford, 2007). As students get comfortable distinguishing factual statements from opinions in their writing, they will be able to build convincing arguments that influence the reader. Here are a few examples of opinion-based writing activities.

Examples of Opinion-Based Writing

◆ Movie, book and theater reviews

◆ Compare and contrast restaurant menus for healthy food

◆ Group writing with a common bias or belief

◆ Advertisement reviews

◆ Personal reflections

♦ Similarities and differences exposés

♦ Editorials

Now let's look at how to put it together for our students.

How the Opinion-Based Writing Intervention Works

1. **Remind students of the various purposes for writing** (e.g., inform, persuade, narrate or tell a story).

2. **Invite students to select a topic that they have a definite opinion on or a belief about** (or you can assign them a topic).

3. **Ask students to share various opinions they have** and why they believe the way they do.

4. **Explain to students the difference between facts and opinions.** Facts are concrete information found from research, while opinions are biases, beliefs, and personal perspectives.

5. **Have students fill out the facts/opinion graphic organizer** to differentiate between fact and opinion in their writing.

6. **Remind students of the paragraph writing strategy** and make sure that students are able to provide supporting sentences that are facts and opinions.

7. **You can ask students to provide one fact and two opinions** as the supporting sentences that make up the body of their paragraphs.

8. **Invite students to swap papers with a peer** and identify the points or perspectives that they find most persuasive.

9. **Once students have confidence writing one persuasive paragraph, they can then add a second paragraph;** some students may be able to write three persuasive paragraphs.

10. **Students who struggle determining the difference between fact and opinion** should work with the teacher in small groups.

ELL Scaffolding

Have ELL students work with a strong partner who can help them distinguish factual statements from opinion statements. If ELL students still struggle, then work with them in small groups to make sure they use factual and opinion-based reasoning to support their arguments when writing.

Why the Opinion-Based Writing Intervention Works

This strategy works because it focuses the process of persuasive writing down to the essential skill of identifying factual statements and opinion statements. Students like sharing their opinions and hearing the opinions and ideas of their peers. As students recognize that opinions are most persuasive when they are connected to statements of fact, they will see their writing improve. Students can follow the paragraph-writing style format for persuasive writing with a slight adjustment. They can begin with a topic sentence. Next, they can provide a sentence of fact followed by a sentence of opinion. They can then repeat this process and provide another statement of fact that supports the topic and follow it up with a sentence of opinion that persuades the reader. Finally, they can write a summarizing sentence to neatly wrap up the paragraph. There are always plenty of topics that will inspire different viewpoints from students. As students write persuasively about these topics, their thinking will develop more fully. Persuasive writers are good thinkers.

Progress Monitoring for the Opinion-Based Writing Intervention

Make sure that students have supporting facts that coincide or coordinate with their opinions. Work with students to use library or Internet resources to find research or facts to support their viewpoint. If students struggle to notice the difference between facts and opinions, work with them one-on-one or in small groups. Once students are able to determine fact from opinion, their persuasive writing will go to the next level.

Writing Intervention #4:
Narrative Story Structure

The first type of writing children typically encounter is narrative—storytelling through a sequence of events. Similarly, the earliest writing for children relies on the personal narrative. The personal narrative allows student to recall, describe, and recount personal life experience. The complement to the personal narrative is the fictional narrative, which gives students permission to imagine, create, and make up stories based on their interests and background knowledge. Narrative story structure is often called story grammar. Mather, Wendling, & Roberts (2009), in addressing writing for struggling students, mention that "story grammar provides students with a framework that can help them produce narrative text" (p. 26). Emphasizing the structure of story grammar for writing, and even reading, can benefit students who come from various cultural backgrounds. As a result, some students may follow an episodic pattern of telling stories that seems to go in circles. Following the story grammar structure can help make sure that these students include important details in their writing. There are five important questions students can ask to help provide them with a complete narrative of the story. The W and H questions are a good way to remember important information when reading a story. In every narrative, the author answers the questions *who, what, when, where, why,* and *how.* These questions are organized into a story structure or story grammar. Here are the W and H questions:

- *Who* is the main character?

- *What* did the main character do?

- *Where* and *when* did the story take place?

- *Why* would we need to know all of that?

- *How* did the main character feel?

- *What* happened at the end of the story?

If students answer these questions, they will know practically everything that happened in the book. They can use this information to write a story. If students struggle to understand this information, teachers can work with them to identify the individual parts of the story and the details surrounding these ideas. The neat thing is that these questions really do work. A group of students started using these W and H questions when reading and found that their comprehension improved so much that they moved right into chapter books. They thought it was easy to answer these questions as a reader, and then began to use the questions to guide their narrative writing.

Common Core State Standards

Grade 4: Write narratives to develop real or imagined experiences or events using effective technique, descriptive details, and clear event sequences.

- Orient the reader by establishing a situation and introducing a narrator and/or characters; organize an event sequence that unfolds naturally.

- Use dialogue and description to develop experiences and events or show the responses of characters to situations.

- Use a variety of transitional words and phrases to manage the sequence of events.

Continued

- Use concrete words and phrases and sensory details to convey experiences and events precisely.
- Provide a conclusion that follows from the narrated experiences or events.

What the Narrative Story Structure Intervention Looks Like

Students need to see the story as a work in progress and the keeper of the story is the reader! The W and H words bring the story into focus and help the reader analyze and comprehend the text and story. A simple outline of each of the components in a story and the W and H words that make up each component helps students see the story as it unfolds. The following story grammar parts connect to the five Ws and the H questions and help students structure their narrative writing effectively.

Main Character and Setting: This character is who the story is about, and the setting tells us where and when the story takes place.

Quest: The quest tells why the story is happening or the motive behind the character.

Actions: The actions show how the main character behaves and how the other characters act in relationship to the main character.

Feelings: The feelings include how people feel or what they learn in the story.

Results/Resolutions: As the story ends, the result or resolution is what happens to the most important character and why it happens.

Knowing these parts of standard story grammar can help struggling students with composition and organization. The Story Grammar Graphic Organizer (Figure 6.5, page 158) can also help students structure their narrative writing.

Narrative stories have a beginning, middle, and end. Narrative writing always tells a story, and can be as simple as the following:

I woke up on a bright, beautiful morning. The bed was messy. I did not want to make it, but then I remembered my momma. I wanted to please her, so I made my bed and cleaned up my room before I left for school. I know my momma thought I was really big to have made my bed all by myself without her asking.

Figure 6.5 Story Grammar Writing Graphic Organizer

Character and Setting:
    Who?
    Where?
    When?

Quest or Objective: Why?

Actions:
    What?
    1.
    2.
    3.

Feelings: How?
Results/Resolutions: What happened in the end?

Here are just a few different types of activities your students can do to develop their narrative writing.

Examples of Narrative Writing

- Personal letter
- Biographical experiences
- Creative writing
- Learning logs
- Storybooks
- Journals
- Personal experiences
- Recall, sequence, and time line

Give students ample opportunities to use their creative writing skills to construct short narratives.

How the Narrative Story Structure Intervention Works

1. **Review with students the key components of a story**—including character, setting, actions, feelings, and conclusions—in a beginning-middle-end format.

2. **Provide models and show examples** of creative and biographical stories that include the Ws. Use your hand as a device for remembering the five Ws.

3. **Ask students to determine *who* might be the main character.** You can also ask them to describe details about the main character or characters.

4. **Next, decide the setting, *where* and *when* the story takes place.** You can also help students understand things in the past or in the future.

5. **Figure out *what* the main character did or what *actions* he or she took.** You can talk with students about what motivated the character to take the actions that he or she did.

6. **Consider *what feelings* the characters may be experiencing.** You can use dialogue to show how people are thinking or feeling. For example, Skeeter said, "Momma, the soup tasted delicious." Momma smiled and said, "I am glad you like it."

7. **Finally, determine *why* the story ends in a certain way.** You can ask why it ended this way, how else it could have ended, and what they learned from the story.

8. **Students can begin by telling if a story is autobiographical** or if it is one that they are personally familiar with.

Figure 6.6 (page 160) shows a narrative story structure for "Stone Soup."

ELL Scaffolding

Using a storybook to start the writing process often works to support students who are not living in a literate environment. Have students fill out the Story Grammar Graphic Organizer and assist ELLs. They then can draw upon that prior experience to participate in writing activities. English Language Learners constantly need to know how to capture what they are reading as the text becomes comprehensible. Learning to organize the information from a narrative or story into discernible chunks using the W words makes it easier for the ELL to check for understanding and follow the lesson as a classroom participant.

Figure 6.6 A Sample Narrative Story Structure

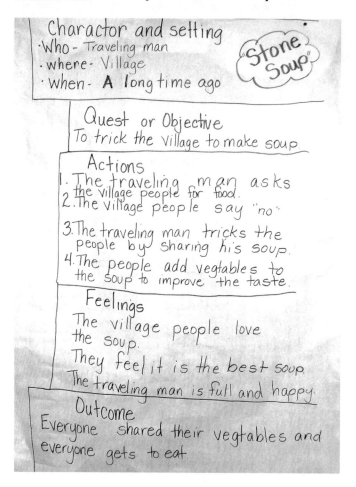

Character and setting
- Who - Traveling man
- where - Village
- when - A long time ago

"Stone Soup"

Quest or Objective
To trick the village to make soup.

Actions
1. The traveling man asks the village people for food.
2. The village people say "no."
3. The traveling man tricks the people by sharing his soup.
4. The people add vegtables to the soup to improve the taste.

Feelings
The village people love the soup.
They feel it is the best soup.
The traveling man is full and happy.

Outcome
Everyone shared their vegtables and everyone gets to eat.

Why the Narrative Story Structure Intervention Works

This strategy works because there are five important questions students should ask themselves to help organize information when they are writing narratives. Using the W questions as a means to structure the story gives young writers a frame for their writing. A simple way to anchor both the W questions and sentence structure follows. It is important for students to learn the Ws, and ask these questions often whenever they write. Asking these five questions will help students consider the important information that readers need to make sense of a variety of types of writing. The graphic organizers with the five parts of story grammar—character and setting, quest, actions, feelings, and results or resolution—will help students see the different parts of standard narrative writing. This intervention helps students' narrative writing and benefits their reading of narrative texts. Understanding this reciprocal relationship between reading and writing narratives is often helpful for students to sustain motivation for reading. Improving narrative writing supports access and understanding of vocabulary, sentence patterns, and fluency. As students follow the five Ws and basic structure of narrative writing, they will be able to add more creativity to their writing.

Progress Monitoring for the Narrative Story Structure Intervention

Review with struggling students that a good story narrative should include details that answer the five Ws (who? what? when? where? and why?) about the experience or event. We use a hand symbol or icon to represent narrative writing. This can be taught as soon as students understand the concept of "story." Students can be easily trained to remember the Ws by using the four fingers and thumb of their hands (Figure 6.7).

Narrative writing should be enjoyable to read. Make sure that students have fun weaving their tale together, yet make sure that they also have the

Figure 6.7 A Trick for Helping Students Remember the Elements of a Narrative

important components of narrative writing. The best way to know if narrative writing is effective is to ask the following questions:

- Can you see someone or something doing this action from a beginning, middle, and ending point?

- Is there a purpose to the story?

- How long does it take for students to start asking these questions automatically of a narrative story or informative text without explicitly being provided the questions or graphic organizer?

A quick five-question quiz at the end of the week about a narrative story or informative text can help determine who comprehends the text and who needs more help.

Writing Intervention #5: Informative/Explanatory Writing Structure

Students learn to write well when they see the connections between what they say, hear, and see. With young children, shared and interactive writing are ways to bridge what students say, hear, and see with how it looks in print. Shared and interactive writing provides the opportunity to practice sight words and see sentence structure. It models the connection between saying and seeing the language in print. All children in the elementary grades need to be involved in frequent guided and independent writing that is information based, experiential, or compelling because of the ideas articulated to support a position. Most writing is audience bound, so the writer must understand who will read the composition for the text to be a success. Informative writing is the basis for all good work in college and in the workplace. It requires the student first to focus, focus, focus on a topic and then to analyze this subject in great detail.

> ## Common Core State Standards
>
> Grade 5: Write informative/explanatory texts to examine a topic and convey ideas and information clearly.
>
> - Introduce a topic clearly, provide a general observation and focus, and group related information logically; include formatting (e.g., headings), illustrations, and multimedia when useful to aiding comprehension.

Continued

- ◆ Develop the topic with facts, definitions, concrete details, quotations, or other information and examples related to the topic.
- ◆ Link ideas within and across categories of information using words, phrases, and clauses (e.g., *in contrast, especially*).
- ◆ Use precise language and domain-specific vocabulary to inform about or explain the topic.
- ◆ Provide a concluding statement or section related to the information or explanation presented.

What the Informative/Explanatory Writing Intervention Looks Like

Informative writing should both inform and provide vivid descriptions about the information provided to the reader. Informing others through writing means students should provide details that will expand the readers' understanding of the topic they chose to write about. Developing skills in description can take a bit of practice for most students. Our students need to be able to identify and use describer words like adjectives and adverbs in their informative writing (Eugene Hammond, 1985). They also will be more descriptive if they add adjective and adverbial prepositional phrases to their writing repertoire. Using prepositional phrases skillfully builds on Listening Intervention #3 about prepositions. Understanding how to use words, phrases, and clauses to describe information is important for elementary students. Students often convey their ideas through writing without knowing exactly what they are trying to accomplish. Consider the three primary methods for adding description to the information in a sentence:

Informative Descriptions

1. Words (adjectives and adverbs)
2. Phrases (prepositional phrases)
3. Clauses (adjective and adverbial clauses)

The first and most common types of describers are adjective and adverb words.

Adjective Describers

- ◆ my <u>favorite</u> baseball mitt
- ◆ the <u>blue</u> race car

- the big fluffy teddy bear
- the kind doctor

Adverb Describers
- ran quickly
- swims awkwardly
- happily skips

Students in grades 3–6 who also become adept at using phrases to add to the descriptions in their informative writing will see their writing become much more effective and much more interesting.

Adjective Phrases
- the man with the two red shoes
- our clock on the desk
- The girl in the cafeteria ate chocolate cake with white frosting.
- My prize was found in a box of sugar-frosted flakes.

Adverbial Phrases
- ran around the track
- fished by the pier
- The volleyball player jumped out of the gym.
- The daisies should be planted between the two trees.

Students in grades 5–6 should begin to use clauses in their writing to create a variety of sentence types (e.g., compound-complex sentences).

Adjective Clauses
- The dog chewed on the big bone that was under the tree.
- The man who ate the entire turkey felt sick.
- Betty is having difficulty finding the pencil that was sitting on the desk.
- Mt. Rainier, which is in Washington, is a beautiful mountain.

Adverbial Clauses
- Did you look under the sink, where we store the caustic chemicals?
- When you get your paycheck, we can go to the store and get you a new television.
- The quarterback ran because the linebacker was trying to tackle him.
- If your lottery ticket pays off, you can splurge for dinner.

Informative writing follows the same pattern provided in Writing Intervention #2: a topic sentence, supporting and descriptive sentences, and a summarizing sentence. Here are a few ideas for different ways to include writing in weekly learning activities.

Examples of Informative Writing

♦ News article

♦ Scientific report

♦ Historical narrative

♦ Mathematical reasoning

♦ Critical analysis essay

♦ Summaries

♦ Informative writing

♦ Biographical essay

♦ How-to writing

How the Informative/Explanatory Intervention Works

1. **Remind students of different purposes for writing** (e.g., inform, persuade, narrate).

2. **Review the paragraph writing style principles** which includes a clear topic sentence, supporting descriptive sentences (at least three), and a summarizing sentence.

3. **Ask students to pick a topic** (or assign them a topic) and to think about the audience they will be providing information to.

4. **Let students know that they want to describe their topic** with lots of detailed description (e.g., describing words, phrases, and clauses).

5. **Review the processes of the paragraph writing strategy** with students so they can remember the basic structure of paragraphs.

6. **Ask students to gather facts and information** that support their topic.

7. **Invite students in grades 3–4 to write a standard five-sentence informative paragraph;** students in grades 5–6 may write more than one five-sentence informative paragraphs.

8. **Ask students to go back after writing and add more description** to each sentence (e.g., adjectives and adverbial words, phrases, and clauses).

9. **Once students are done with their informative writing, they can read their writing to a peer,** and the peer can write down and comment on the description they liked in the writing.

10. **One final way to practice informative writing would be to ask students to describe various things in the classroom.** Students should write vivid details about the items their sentences describe. The more adjectives, adjective phrases, and clauses used, the better.

ELL Scaffolding

For many English Language Learners, their native language may place describing words after the word being described (e.g., *car blue* instead of *blue car*). Discussing how words, phrases, and clauses are used in their native language can help them see how to use and structure descriptive language in English.

Why the Informative/Explanatory Writing Intervention Works

This strategy works because it helps students understand one major purpose of writing and helps them become better writers. Every student wants to be able to more creatively describe the world around him or her through writing. This strategy helps students see the specific components of writing that informs and describes (adjectives, adverbs, adjective and adverbial phrases, and adjective and adverbial clauses). Students will be more engaged and more excited to go through the process of informing through writing if they see that their skills as writers are developing. Knowing the structures of describing will give students more confidence as writers. Being descriptive is a skill that will help students in every aspect of their writing. Good writing is full of details that use words to describe the intriguing aspects of the topic. Informative writing can sometimes be a little dry. Effective writers use description to make it interesting.

Progress Monitoring for the Informative/Explanatory Writing Intervention

Work with students one-on-one or in small groups to see if they can identify the structure of descriptive writing. For example, give them a short paragraph and have them identify adjective words, adverb words, prepositional phrases that describe, and clauses that describe the information being presented. After students are able to identify different types of descriptions when they read, ask them to write out sentences describing subjects and verbs. They should practice each skill of words, phrases, and clauses separately until they can do it with little prompting. Make sure that students are able to provide the following methods of describing:

♦ **Describer words:** Adjectives and adverbs answer *what kind?* And adverbs answer *where?* and *when?*

♦ **Describer phrases**: Adjective phrases also answer *what kind?* Adverbial phrases also answer *where?* and *when?*

♦ **Describer clauses**: Adjective clauses are introduced with words like *that, which,* and *who.* Adverbial clauses are introduced with words like *when, because, if, as, where,* and *although.*

Have fun with your students as you play with the words, phrases, and clauses that describe informative writing.

Summing It Up

Students in grades 3–6 need frequent opportunities to express their thinking through writing each week. Consistent and constant intervention support in student writing will make a big difference in our classrooms. Students need explicit modeling and instruction in the key processes that develop effective writing and writers. Thinking improves as our students write aloud and reflect on how they communicate their various ideas. As students master writing the narrative story, they will better identify the five Ws that outline the *who, what, where, when,* and *why* of writing. Learning to write effective paragraphs is important for students in grades 3–6. Informative writing will prepare students once they leave elementary school and enter middle school, high school, and beyond. Our students' writing will improve as they learn to use descriptive words, phrases, and clauses. Students who are provided opportunities to engage in persuasive writing are better able to distinguish facts from opinions. Writing is the capstone literacy skill. Good writers are good readers, good speakers, better listeners, and better thinkers. Making sure that every student receives interventions and opportunities to improve their writing will produce tremendous results.

Reflection

1. How much time each week is devoted to engaging students in writing strategies that will develop their cognitive processes and thinking skills?

2. Do your students actively negotiate with the author when they read, and do they negotiate effectively with the audience when they write?

7

Implementing Strategies That Work

"Leadership and Learning are indispensable to one another."

—President John F. Kennedy

> Destiny whistles quietly down the walkway on her way to the library. She is looking forward to getting some new books from the library. She is now reading chapter books. Her sense of accomplishment as a reader has opened up her appreciation for school. At some point this year, her outlook on reading and learning changed. Her confidence to embrace the challenges of school has quietly increased. She feels the support from her teacher and knows she will receive the help she needs. The daily small-group instruction and extra attention in class has definitely made a big difference. Her ability to infer and make predictions has increased. The number of words she knows has grown significantly. Her math skills are stronger. She enjoys participating in "academic talk" with her friends in class. She likes to write even though she knows she still makes a lot of spelling mistakes. Instead of dreading school, Destiny finds that it has become a pleasure to read. Destiny is a confident learner who is whistling a new tune and appreciates everything that her teacher has done for her this year.

It is important that we integrate and implement intervention strategies that work into our daily activities. Providing consistent interventions that support content area learning (e.g., language arts, science, social studies, math) adds up in so many ways. As our friend and colleague Brad Wilcox says about interventions, "A little bit every day, is better than a lot in May." As we consistently add more intervention strategies to our daily routine, we will soon expand our intervention repertoire. We will be prepared to meet the demands that our diverse students bring with them to school. The great thing about intervention strategies that work is they can be applied to a variety of content areas. The reading, writing, speaking, and listening strategies can be used in language arts, science, math, social studies, and a variety of other subjects.

Interventions

Our educational system needs an intervention if it is to truly educate a populace that can fully participate in the freedoms of being American. Without an education in this global economy, unsuccessful students lose choices for the future; they literally become less free. If we are successful in educating all children to their highest abilities, they will enjoy access, and the right to engage, in the life of their choice. Intervention needs to start as early as possible, especially for our students who come to school from a low socioeconomic background. Richard Weissbourd, an education researcher, articulates the need to realize that many high-needs children are not disruptive; many high-need youth have "quiet" problems that often fly under their schools' radar. Our students in grades 3–6 need and deserve intervention strategies that work. The preceding chapters provided 25 power-packed strategies that you can use in Tier I and Tier II intervention activities. These strategies help students because they increase the level of access, engagement, structure, and meaning that they definitely need to succeed. Interventions are necessary when students don't tag, understand, or "get" new information or demands for new thinking. The need for intervention, the lack of connecting, must be transcended and shifted so students have the ability to think about, write about, articulate, and problem solve their understanding of what they are learning. We can improve the quality and the techniques or tactics utilized in first instruction. It is possible to reduce the incidence of students requiring intervention. However, the most important aspect of this process is to reduce the stigma too often associated with embracing help—whether as a student or a teacher—and accept the challenge to truly create the conditions for all students to succeed.

Adding Arrows to Your Arsenal

As we add more intervention strategies to our instructional quiver, we will be prepared with the arrows in our arsenal that we need to help all students be effective learners. Every teacher needs to expand his or her instructional repertoire. The teacher's instructional repertoire is the quiver that holds the arrows that can get at the heart of student learning. The arrows are the teacher's intervention strategies that may be used to increase student learning. Some arrows or intervention strategies will work with some students, while other arrows or intervention strategies will work with others. The key is to have enough intervention arrows in our arsenal to meet the needs of all our students. If we have a variety of intervention strategies that we can effectively direct towards learning targets, then we will be able to redirect the learning success for our students.

Access: Many students face roadblocks to their education because they have challenges that limit their access to information. Language and literacy experiences are the key issues that affect a student's ability to access the important information provided at school. For many, the language issues arise because English is their second language. For other students, the language issues occur because students come from low socioeconomic backgrounds. Poverty and its dramatic consequences affect language and learning.

Engaging: Students direct their attention and their energy to things that are engaging. As they interact with information in ways that are engaging, they are more likely to extend and elaborate on their learning. Most engagement requires an emotional response within the learning process. Hooking students to learn is the primary task of sustaining an engaged classroom.

Structure: The key to instruction is developing students' internal structures so that they can participate successfully. Some students naturally have the internal resources to create these structures, or they have support at home to help create these structures. At the same time, many students lack the understanding of how to develop structures that will benefit them now as well as in the future. All students need the strategies that support an academic foundation and require the structures that will help them build an academic framework of learning.

Meaning: Students develop meaning in two ways. They develop meaning externally by negotiating with others about what things mean to others and internally by clarifying their own understanding of the material being learned. As students listen, read, speak, and write, they are able to negotiate with their teachers, peers, and book authors regarding meaning and their own personal understanding. At the same time, students develop meaning internally by negotiating with new information they receive. As they process the information, they monitor and adjust their learning and how it affects their worldview. Learning changes people. A child in third grade learning the multiplication table becomes a different student when the math facts are known to a high level of automaticity. Learning helps us evolve in our understanding of how the world operates and how we might fit into that world successfully.

Without intervention strategies that work, many of our students will struggle and may become high-risk students, potentially becoming one of the 1.2 million students that drop out of school each year. When we effectively use intervention strategies that work for our 3–6 students, we can positively impact results. Learning outcomes and life outcomes can be altered dramatically in positive ways. We can literally change the trajectory of a child's life by ensuring their success at school.

Repeated Practice with Intervention Strategies

Our students need to engage in intervention strategies at least six to twelve times for them to become proficient in the strategy. Burns (2004) emphasizes that new strategies benefit students most when the students go through all five stages of learning.

1. Acquisition
2. Proficiency and fluency
3. Maintenance and practice
4. Generalization to other experiences
5. Adaptation to new learning opportunities

When students get to the fifth level, adaption, they own the strategy and can use their newfound knowledge and skills effectively in a variety of learning situations. Applying the strategies in this book once or twice with our students will fall short of truly intervening academically for our students.

Interventions for those who are addicts follow a twelve-step process, and students who struggle in school may need twelve times with each of these strategies in whole-group, small-group, and even one-on-one settings to build the internal capacity to learn effectively at grade-level. Integrate the strategies with content topics that will expand their knowledge and their capacity to learn in the future.

Language Foundation = Relationships

Language provides the means for understanding and describing the many ways we think about the world. One of the basic functions of language is to enable people to engage in social interaction where we can express our thinking. Language allows us to express our thoughts, ideas, and perspectives at the same time we are able to receive others thoughts, ideas, and perspectives. Thinking in academic terms requires words and language that can convey the complex, organized, and connected ideas associated with learning. Academic language provides us with the educational currency to share our intelligence and thinking with others. Consider the following examples of academic language as they are used to support three different types of thinking: creative, critical, and metacognitive. Academic language that emphasizes creative thinking includes powerful words like *discover*, *generate*, *construct*, and *develop*. Academic language that emphasizes critical thinking includes *analyze*, *determine*, and *evaluate*. Academic language that emphasizes metacognitive thinking includes *reflect*, *consider*, *ponder*, and *review*.

The more language we know and understand, the easier it is to pick up, process, and produce more language. Helping students develop the ability to acquire language in many different subjects is an important responsibility of our schools. Acquisition of language starts before school even begins, and it will continue as long as we are actively learning. Language and learning go together. We use language to describe our learning, and in turn learning strengthens our ability to acquire more language. Language provides the basic building blocks for constructing the knowledge structures that help us organize and connect ideas together. Knowledge structures are the key ideas and connections that hold our conceptual knowledge together. Academic language provides the basic building blocks for constructing academic knowledge structures. As we learn new academic language terms, we are able to receive additional understanding of conceptual knowledge and create within us knowledge structures. As we learn new academic language terms, we are also able to express our understanding of conceptual knowledge and identify within ourselves the individual building blocks of our knowledge structures. These academic knowledge structures, then, serve as the background knowledge that we can use to build upon for future learning. Knowledge structures help us organize our own thinking and make sense of the conceptual thinking of others.

Academic language acts as a key that helps to unlock a student's academic thinking, academic literacy, and academic learning. Students who struggle with the literacy demands of speaking, listening, reading, and writing most often lack the academic language that will lead to academic success. Fillmore (2004) points out the importance of academic language quite clearly: "What is it that differentiates students who make it from those who do not? This list is long, but very prominent among the factors is mastery of academic language" (p. 4).

Literacy Framework = Negotiating

In a country that is becoming more diverse in culture and languages, developing academic literacy is becoming an increasingly important issue in our schools. Moxley and Taylor (2006) share a comprehensive view that "literacy is defined as listening, viewing, thinking, speaking, writing, and reading…" (p. 102). As academic language and the precise thinking that goes with it are infused in the key processes of reading, writing, viewing, listening, and speaking, learning becomes grounded in a firm foundation. This academic language foundation then serves as a solid footing for creating the academic literacy frameworks that support a variety of academic content knowledge. Developing literacy in core content areas creates confidence for students. Whether it is in mathematics or science, in language arts or history, literacy provides students with the skills for lifelong learning. Understanding the types of academic language, the structures of academic language, and the methods for developing academic language are necessary skills that all learners need in today's schools.

Language is one of the key characteristics that make us uniquely human. The ability to communicate using symbols gives us the means to share intelligence and learn from others. Language has two primary modes or purposes: expressive and receptive. We typically engage in the expressive use of language by speaking and writing. We typically engage in the receptive use of language by listening and reading. Literacy is defined in simple terms as "the ability to read, write, speak, and listen." As we effectively learn to develop both the expressive modes of language (speaking and writing) and the receptive modes of language (listening and reading), we develop literacy. In a literate culture, our ideas and learning are transmitted and preserved in writing.

Learning Finishing Work = Organizing

The further one goes in their education, the greater the academic language demands and the higher the level of literacy skills needed for success. Most people talk about the significant gaps that exist among learners in America's schools and label these as achievement gaps. The research shows that the achievement gap finds its genesis in a literacy gap. The literacy gap begins in many cases before students even start school, and without coordinated efforts by school leaders, this gap consistently widens as students continue their schooling (Barone, 2006). Bridging this gap will take the combined efforts of students, classroom teachers, site leaders, and district administrators to change results and create more equitable social opportunities for all learners.

Recognizing the impact of these facts may astonish everyone except those classroom teachers who face the challenges of engaging these students on a daily basis. The solutions to these increasing dilemmas require the awareness and collaboration of all educational leaders. Understanding academic language and the instructional strategies that support academic literacy will provide teachers with the ability to integrate learning for all students. Integrating academic language and academic literacy in school will increase students' abilities to be more successful in all of the core content areas of mathematics, language arts, science, and social studies. Content-area teachers and school leaders stand at the crossroads of transforming education for economically disadvantaged students who lack so many vital language and literacy skills.

Explicitly providing academic language instruction will improve our students' ability to develop literacy and effectively meet the increasing demands of school. As we work together to more fully develop academic language and support academic literacy, we will begin to fill in the language gaps and bridge the achievement gap so that all of our students can become successful, prepared citizens in the global economy of today as well as tomorrow. Academic language is both the foundation and the framework for scaffolding lifelong learning and literacy for all students. If consistent high-quality instruction truly provides the scaffolding for student success in school, then academic language provides both the building blocks and the conceptual cement for creating a foundation and framework of academic success and professional progress.

Professional Learning Communities and RTI

Professional learning communities (PLCs) are an important means to creating structure and support for educational reform, organizational learning, and analyzing data. To do this, teachers need to be in a collaborative process, a professional learning community (DuFour, 2003). Working and learning with colleagues helps teachers develop the skills and abilities to use and apply data. Each member of the collaborative team contributes to dialogues, shares real time experiences, and plans for the high-need students. This "real world" lens helps teachers interpret data, validate findings, and make planning decisions. The PLC allows teachers to collaborate and develop interim and formative assessments. Assessment literacy, alignment to standards, decision-making processes, data skills, and strategy identification are the strategies used by a collaborative team.

Collaboration does not happen magically because professionals are given dedicated time every week to get work done together. Collaboration time does not make a "team," nor does time set aside make that team efficacious. Collaboration is initiated by a group because of its attraction to a shared mission or belief in a common goal. Attraction brings people together and initiates an emotional process. Coming together, people begin a type of "dance"; they start to develop a way to be in sync by setting norms and protocol for interaction and communication. The experience of setting norms and being attracted by, or sharing, a common mission initiates rapport, which is the foundation of permission—the time in a relationship when it becomes OK to ask questions, look for similarities or differences, and establish emotional connections—and from this point individuals develop influence. Influence is the basis of collaboration; it fosters trust and respect, places value on shared work, and ultimately puts teams in the position to reflect meaningfully on their practice.

Collaboration generates the conditions that foster empowerment. The more a team believes together, the more it will achieve together. Interestingly, when teachers believe that they can do the work, perceive that they have enough available resources, and deem that there is adequate peer/professional/supervisory support for their work, they are more likely to do the work required and more capable of accomplishing the work and changing their practice to accommodate whatever needs to be done. Alcoholics Anonymous, Wayne Gretsky, Tiger Woods—they all believe it, too.

School-level mechanisms can provide incentives to support the PLC process, including support for data inquiry, instructional improvement, and continuous improvement. Recognition of hard work can prompt the team to learn and grow. DuFour and Eaker (1998) recommend these strategies to foster student achievement through the use of professional learning communities.

Supporting Implementation

Given the opportunity, teachers can develop the capacity to implement new strategies and reframe instruction, but they must understand what needs to be done. The following steps can be taken to ensure effective implementation:

- Start with the standard. Explain the verb—the action reflects the learning that will be experienced. Take three to five minutes to find out background knowledge. Use a classic T-chart. On the left, write *What I Already Know*. On the right, write *How I Use This Information/Skill or Why This Is Important*. This is a quick way to start the dialogue about the standard, and it is a great way to make a mind map—of how this standard or content connects to other information and skills.

- Describe the strategy in plain terms that everyone can understand.

- Describe the series of steps students must take in order to use the strategy successfully.

- Explain how the strategy addresses the objective.

- Engage students in the strategy six to twelve times so that they can become proficient in the strategy.

- Describe results in understated terms.

To implement each strategy well, students will benefit from prioritizing or ranking the instructional strategies. Make sure that the new practices garner gains in achievement. No one knows what will work for every child, so a certain amount of experimentation is necessary. However, use strategies that are science based and have high effect sizes.

Increasing Capacity

Building capacity within our school organizations is important for us as teachers and for our students. As we expand the number of strategies in our instructional repertoire, we increase our capacity, and as we introduce our students to new strategies, they will increase their capacity as well. Strengthening capacity means leveraging human capital, social capital, and organizational capital. Human capital includes knowledge, commitment, and the disposition to improve. Social capital relies on professional networks, trust, and collaboration. Organizational capital refers to the local organization's capacity to mobilize resources such as time, staffing, and materials for implementing change.

Building capacity, the phenomenon of "growing" know-how, is the responsibility of any dynamic classroom and school organization that wants to sustain both its mission to reach all kids and its ability to remain responsive to changing needs. These two truths underscore this important premise related to capacity: 1) Change is the only constant; nothing ever stays the same. 1) No organization is impervious to change, which requires that everyone must embrace change and leverage the ability to build capacity—new skills, strategies, and solutions—in response to demands of an evolving system. Intervention strategies provide additional, flexible ways for reaching students and building the capacity to learn for our students. As we increase our own capacity to use additional strategies effectively, we will be able to better meet the needs of our students, so that they will be prepared for the challenges of the 21st century.

Creating Sustainability

We want to create sustainable results that will work consistently in our classroom and will benefit our students into the future. Providing effective intervention strategies is important for students, and with it we also need to embrace organizational strategies that support effective learning. In addition to needing high-quality intervention strategies, student achievement can be supported by the following nine practices:

1. high expectations (These can be expressed only if the average or normal expectation is first explained; then provide the challenge to exceed the norm, and describe what that would mean.);
2. clear goals that are articulated, posted, and tested for understanding;
3. high levels of classroom collaboration coupled with structured peer interactions;
4. curriculum aligned to standards and assessments so that the intended is delivered and attained;
5. focused professional development (PD) linked explicitly to the topics and skills meant to help now; PD is responsive and answers immediate problems but also builds skills for the future;

6. teacher efficacy, where teachers have the confidence they know the specific interventions that will support student learning for each and every student;

7. monitored instruction via walk-throughs, observations, and requests for peer feedback as well as adjustments made to instruction to ensure that all students have access to concepts, context, and content;

8. site leadership that guides pedagogical inquiry and facilitates the overall work and the reflection of practice,

9. students and teachers using their voices and choices to support learning for every student.

As we think about building capacity, we should also recognize our capacity to absorb new learning at any given time. The intervention strategies provided in this book are organized for easy reference so that you can refer back to them as needs arise in the future. While you might start today with the four or five strategies that will help your students the most, you can always return and review the strategies, tips, and suggestions to help your students in future situations. So, as the capacity of our instructional repertoire increases, then we will also see the capacity of our students' learning increase.

Summing It Up

Thank you for choosing to intervene in positive ways on behalf of your students. The work you do each and every day makes a difference. As teachers, we need to expand our instructional repertoires. Our intervention toolkits reflect the years of practice; they are the skills, strategies, and solutions that we use to respond to the difficulties students present while trying to access content, engage in context, and learn new concepts, which results in new data to be verified, information to be checked, knowledge to be embraced, and wisdom to be celebrated. As our classrooms fill up with more and more students who struggle to keep up with grade-level standards, our capacity to meet our students' needs must also increase.

Whenever our students are unable to connect or assimilate learning, then new answers are needed. This is the gap where "intervention answers" are required. These answers are the instructional, experiential, and emotional interventions that will provide students access, engagement, structure, and meaning to connect with the classroom, the text, the assignment, or the test. The strategies we use to reach all students to help them develop their skills and become proficient life-long learners are a big part of what we do every day. English Language Learners (ELLs), students from poverty (Title I), and struggling readers benefit from the personalized interventions that we provide them so they can grasp the knowledge and skills to succeed academically. Teaching is so much more than making sure our students get the right answer on one test in May. We have to make sure that they can think for the rest of the year and write about their thoughts, share their perceptions, and make informed choices. The relationships and emotional interactions we develop in the process are a kind of a footprint that will be left because of the time spent on the planet. As we add strategic arrows to our intervention quivers, we will be better prepared to meet all of the demands that students bring to our classrooms. Students need help developing their listening, reading, math, speaking, spelling, and writing strategies. We hope that you enjoyed all of the strategies contained in this second volume of our RTI Intervention series. As you regularly implement these interventions in your classroom, we know that you will enjoy the strategies and your students will appreciate the support. Enjoy the journey!

Reflection

1. Which intervention strategies will you implement in your classroom to make sure every student succeeds?
2. How will you share these interventions with your fellow teachers and colleagues?

Appendix A

Academic Language Grade-Level Lists

Third grade

1. academic
2. achieve
3. as
4. assemble
5. assess
6. attitude
7. attribute
8. award
9. balance
10. believe
11. bias
12. chart
13. clarify
14. code
15. communicate
16. concept
17. confidence
18. control
19. core
20. cycle
21. data

22. decision
23. demonstrate
24. despite
25. detect
26. elect
27. emotional
28. employ
29. eventually
30. exercise
31. experiment
32. explore
33. foundation
34. frequently
35. global
36. grant
37. immediately
38. instead
39. integrate
40. intelligence
41. introduce
42. invite

43. level
44. mental
45. method
46. model
47. objectives
48. organize
49. perhaps
50. phase
51. portfolio
52. primary
53. profession
54. project
55. publish
56. punish
57. quality
58. quantity
59. reflect
60. region
61. report
62. self-control
63. settle

64. sketch
65. social
66. source
67. supply

68. system
69. theme
70. train
71. transport

72. trend
73. tutor
74. until
75. while

Fourth grade

1. additionally
2. adjust
3. afterwards
4. anticipate
5. apply
6. approve
7. assist
8. attitude
9. authority
10. character
11. college
12. concept
13. conserve
14. culture
15. curriculum
16. defend
17. devote
18. dialogue
19. document
20. eliminate
21. emphasize
22. equality
23. evaluate
24. evidence
25. examine

26. exchange
27. exercise
28. exhibit
29. express
30. feedback
31. fine-tune
32. for example
33. frame
34. frequently
35. gauge
36. host
37. importantly
38. inform
39. inspire
40. lecture
41. license
42. lighten
43. log
44. mean
45. mention
46. motivate
47. nurture
48. operate
49. portfolio
50. prevent

51. principles
52. produce
53. range
54. rather
55. reality
56. reason
57. reduce
58. relate
59. release
60. replace
61. represent
62. research
63. result
64. retain
65. schedule
66. signify
67. similarly
68. sometimes
69. stimulate
70. strengthen
71. structure
72. supervise
73. technology
74. translate
75. update

Fifth grade

1. approach
2. automatically
3. besides
4. bias
5. challenge
6. collaborate
7. collate
8. commit
9. compile
10. conclude
11. conduct
12. conscious
13. consequence
14. content
15. enable
16. engage
17. environment
18. equip
19. establish
20. even though
21. ever since
22. expand
23. expert
24. explain
25. extend
26. feature
27. fee
28. forecast
29. furthermore
30. in order that
31. influence
32. inspect
33. install
34. insure
35. involve
36. issue
37. launch
38. maintain
39. manage
40. maximize
41. meanwhile
42. medical
43. narrate
44. navigate
45. on the other hand
46. opinion
47. perfect
48. preserve
49. primarily
50. probability
51. reason
52. refine
53. remodel
54. repair
55. reserve
56. respond
57. restrict
58. retain
59. sample
60. screen
61. series
62. simplify
63. still
64. straighten
65. submit
66. surely
67. symbolic
68. synthesize
69. system
70. technical
71. thus
72. transform
73. uncover
74. unify
75. upgrade

Sixth grade

1. abstract
2. accumulate
3. assume
4. boost
5. career
6. certainly
7. cite
8. civil
9. clause
10. component
11. conceptualize
12. concrete
13. console
14. contact
15. contrastingly

16. currently
17. dedicate
18. defer
19. diagnose
20. differentiate
21. discharge
22. effective
23. efficient
24. enlarge
25. enlist
26. even when
27. expand
28. extract
29. file
30. filter
31. finalize
32. habit
33. initially
34. institute
35. integrate

36. likelihood
37. localize
38. logic
39. mediate
40. mentor
41. merge
42. metaphor
43. modify
44. moral
45. notify
46. obtain
47. occupation
48. perceive
49. perhaps
50. preside
51. reaction
52. reference
53. regulate
54. relevance
55. reorganize

56. response
57. restore
58. scheme
59. scope
60. sequentially
61. significantly
62. simultaneously
63. spearhead
64. specialize
65. survey
66. tense
67. therefore
68. transfer
69. transmit
70. undertake
71. unveil
72. value
73. version
74. viewpoint
75. witness

Academic Language
Graphic Organizer

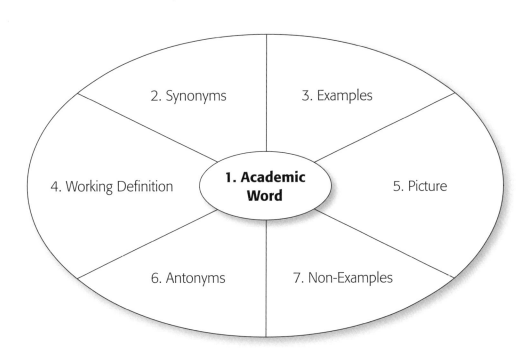

References

Alliance for Excellent Education (2009). Understanding high school graduation rates in the United States. Retrieved from http://www.all4ed.org/files/National_wc.pdf.

Barone, D. (2006). *Narrowing the literacy gap: What works in high poverty schools.* New York, NY: Guilford Press.

Barone, D., Mallette, M. & Hong Xu, S. (2005). *Teaching early literacy: Development, assessment, & instruction.* New York, NY: Guilford Press.

Baumann, J. & Kaamenui, E. (2004). *Reading vocabulary: Research to practice.* New York, NY: Guilford Press.

Bearne, E., Dombey, H., & Grainger, T. (2003). *Classroom interactions in literacy.* New York, NY: McGraw-Hill International.

Benard, B. (2004). *Resiliency: What we have learned.* San Francisco, CA: WestEd.

Bernhardt, V. & Hebert, C. (2011). *Response to intervention and continuous school improvement: Using data, vision, and leadership to design, implement, and evaluate a school-wide prevention system.* Larchmont, NY: Eye On Education.

Brown-Chidsey, R. & Cummings, J. (2007). *Assessment for intervention: A problem solving approach.* New York, NY: Guilford Press.

Burns, M. (2004). Empirical analysis of drill ratio research: Refining the instructional level for drill tasks. *Remedial and Special Education, Vol. 25, Number 3.*

Cain, K. & Oakhill, J. (2007). *Children's comprehension problems in oral and written languages.* New York, NY: Guilford Press.

California English Language Development Test (CELDT). Retrieved on 12/1/11 from http://www.cde.ca.gov/ta/tg/el/

Callela, T. (2004). *Greek and Latin roots grades, 4–8: Teaching vocabulary to improve reading comprehension.* Huntington Beach, CA: Creative Teaching Press.

Cantone, K. (2010). *Code-switching in bilingual children.* New York, NY: Springer.

Charlesworth, R. (2011). *Experiences in math for young children.* Florence, KY: Wadsworth Publishing.

Clifford, T. (2007). *Crafting opinion and persuasive papers: For teachers of developing writers.* Gainesville, FL: Maupin House Publishers.

Colorín Colorado (2007). Using Cognates to Develop Comprehension in English. Retrieved from http://www.colorincolorado.org/article/14307/

Cosby, B. & Poussaint, A. (2007). *Come on, people: On the path from victims to victors.* Nashville, TN: Thomas Nelson.

Cunningham, & Allington, (1999). *Classrooms that work: They can all read and write.* Boston, MA: Allyn & Bacon.

Dictionary.com

Diehl, H. & Nettles, D. (2010). *Strategies for powerful comprehension instruction: It takes more than mentioning.* Huntington Beach, CA: Shell Education.

Donohue, L. (2007). *Guided listening: A framework for using read-aloud and other oral language.* Ontario, Canada: Pembroke Publishers Limited.

DuFour, R. (2003). Building a professional learning community: For system leaders, it means allowing autonomy within defined parameters. *The School Administrator.* March 8, 2008.

Empson, S. B. & Levi, L. (2011). *Extending children's mathematics: Fractions and decimals.* Portsmouth, NH: Heinemann.

Fillmore, L. (2004). The role of language in academic development. In excerpts from a presentation by Lily Wong Fillmore at the Closing the Achievement Gap for EL Students conference. Santa Rosa: CA: Sonoma County Office of Education. Retrieved from http://www.scoe.k12.ca.us/aiming_high/docs/AH_language.pdf

Fisher, D., Rothenberg, C. & Frey, N. (2008). *Content area conversations: How to plan discussion based lessons for diverse learners.* Alexandria, VA: ASCD.

Fountas & Pinnell (1996). *Guided reading: Good first teaching for all children.* Portsmouth, NH: Heinemann.

Fullan, M. (2001). *The New Meaning of Education Change, 3rd Edition.* New York, NY: Teachers College Press.

Grant, T. & Littlejohn, G. (2005). *Teaching green the elementary years: Hands on learning in grades K–5.* Gabriola Island, BC: New Society Publishers.

Hammond, E. (1985). *Informative writing.* Columbus, OH: McGraw-Hill.

Harry, B., & Klingner, J. (2006). *Why are so many minority students in special education? Understanding race and disability in schools.* New York, NY: Teachers College Press.

Hart, B. & Risley, T. (2003). The early catastrophe: The 30 million word gap by age 3. *American Educator, 22,* 4–9.

Hattie, J. (2009). *Visible learning: A synthesis of over 800 meta-analyses relating to achievement.* New York, NY: Routledge.

Haven, K. & Ducey, M. (2007). *Crash course in story-telling*. Santa Barbara, CA: Libraries Unlimited.

Haven, K. (2004). *Get it Write: Creating lifelong writers, from expository to narrative*. Portsmouth, NH: Heinemann.

Hirsch, E. (2006). The case for bringing content into the language arts block and for a knowledge-rich curriculum core for all children. *American Educator. 30(1)*, 8–17.

Hirsch, E. (2003). Reading comprehension requires knowledge of words and the world: Scientific insights into the fourth-grade reading slump and the nation's stagnant comprehension scores. *American Educator. 27(1)*, 10–29.

Hoffman, T. (2011). *Prepositional placement in English: A usage based approach*. New York, NY: Cambridge University Press.

Honig, B., Diamond, L. & Gutlohn, L. (2000). *Teaching reading: Sourcebook for kindergarten through eighth grade*. Novato, CA: Arena Press.

Hoy, W. & Miskel, C. (2002). *Theory and Research in Educational Administration*. Charlotte, NC: Information Age Publishing.

Irvin, J., Meltzer, J., & Dukes, M. (2007). Taking action on adolescent literacy: an implementation guide for school leaders. p. 268. Alexandria, VA: ASCD.

Isurin, L., Winford, D. & deBot, K., eds. (2009). *Multidisciplinary approaches to code switching*. Amsterdam: John Benjamins.

Ivey, G. & Fisher, D. (2006). *Creating literacy-rich schools for adolescents*. Alexandria, VA: ASCD.

Johnson, E. & Karns, M. (2011). *RTI Strategies That work in the K–2 classroom*. Larchmont, NY: Eye On Education.

Johnson, E. (2009). *Academic language! Academic literacy! A guide for K–12 educators*. Thousand Oaks, CA: Corwin Press.

Kasper, L. & Babbitt, M. (2000). *Content-based college ESL instruction*. New York, NY: Routledge.

Kenney, J., Hancewicz, E., Heuer, L., Metsisto, D. & Tuttle, C. (2005). Reading in the mathematics classroom. In *Literacy strategies for improving mathematics instruction*. (Chapter 2). Alexandria, VA: ASCD

Kerry, T. (1982). *Effective questioning: A teaching skills workbook*. Basingstoke: Macmillan Education.

Killen, R. (2006). *Effective teaching strategies*. Florence, KY: Cengage Learning.

Kruse, D. (2009). *Thinking strategies for the inquiry classroom*. Melbourne, AU: Curriculum Corporation.

Langer, J. (1985). Children's sense of genre: A study of performance on parallel reading and writing tasks. *Written Communication, 2, 2*, 157–188.

Lave, J. & Wenger, E. (1991). *Situational learning: Legitimate peripheral participation*. New York, NY: Cambridge University Press.

Lems, K., Miller, L. & Soro, T. (2009). *Teaching reading to English language learners: Insights from linguistics*. New York, NY: Guilford Press.

Levi, D. (2010). *Group dynamics for teams*. Thousand Oaks, CA: Sage Publications.

Maanum, J. (2009). *The general educator's guide to special education*. Thousand Oaks, CA: Corwin Press.

Marzano, R., Pickering, D. & Pollock, J. (2001). *Classroom instruction that works: Research-based strategies for increasing student achievement*. Alexandria, VA: ASCD.

Mather, N., Wendling, B. & Roberts, R. (2009). *Writing assessment and instruction for students with learning disabilities*. San Francisco, CA: Jossey Bass.

Moats, L. (2000). *Speech to print: Language essentials for teachers*. Baltimore, MD: Brookes.

Morrow, L., Gambrell, L. & Duke N. (2011). *Best practices in literacy instruction, fourth edition*. New York, NY: Guilford Press.

Moxley, D. & Taylor, R. (2006). *Literacy coaching: A handbook for school leaders*. Thousand Oaks, CA: Corwin Press.

Nagin, C. (2003). *Because writing matters: Improving student writing in our schools*. San Francisco, CA: Jossey Bass.

Nagy, W. & Anderson, R. (1984). How many words are there in printed English? *Reading Research Quarterly, 19*, 304–330.

National Mathematics Advisory Panel (2008). Final Report: Foundations for success: The Final Report of the National Mathematics Advisory Panel. U.S. Department of Education: Washington, DC.

National Council of Teachers of Mathematics. (2000). Principles and standards for school mathematics. Reston, VA: Author.

National Governors Association Center for Best Practices and the Council of Chief State School Officers. The Common Core State Standards. Retrieved from http://www.corestandards.org

Nation, P. (2001). *Learning vocabulary in another language*. New York, NY: Cambridge University Press.

Neuman, S. & Dickson, D. (2010). *Handbook of early literacy research, third edition*. New York, NY: Guilford Press.

Nobre, K. & Coull, J. (2010). *Attention and time*. Oxford, England: Oxford University Press.

Olson, C. & Land, R. (2007). A cognitive strategies approach to reading and writing. *Research in the Teaching of English, Volume 41, Number 3*, 269, February 2007.

PBS.org/teacherline: http://www.pbs.org/teachers/_files/pdf/Microsoft%20 Word_FINALMathTipDoc.pdf

Pearson, P., Hiebert, E., & Kamil, M. (2007). Vocabulary assessment: What we know and what we need to learn. *Reading Research Quarterly, 42*, 282–296.

Quinn, A. (1993). *Figures of speech: 60 ways to turn a phrase.* Davis, CA: Hermagora Press.

Ramey, C. T., & Ramey, S. L. (1998). Early intervention and early experience. *American Psychologist, 53,* 109–120.

Rathvon, N. (2008). *Effective school interventions: Evidence-based strategies for improving student outcomes. Second edition.* New York, NY: Guilford Press.

Reading/language arts framework for California public schools: Kindergarten through grade twelve. (2007). Sacramento, CA: CDE Press.

Resnick, L. (1988). Treating mathematics as an ill-structured discipline. In R. Charles & E. Silver (Eds.), *The teaching and assessing of mathematical problem solving* (pp. 32-60). Hillsdale, NJ: Lawrence Erlbaum Associates.

Riccomini, P. & Witzel, B. (2009). *Response to intervention in math.* Thousand Oaks, CA: Corwin Press.

Rock, D. (2009). *The brain at work: Strategies for overcoming distraction, regaining focus, and working smarter all day long.* New York, NY: Harper Business.

Romano, T. (1987). *Clearing the way: Working with teenage writers.* Portsmouth, NH: Heinemann.

Rubenstein, R. (2001). Mental mathematics beyond the middle school. *Mathematics Teacher, 94(6),* 442.

Scanlon, D., Anderson, K., & Sweeney, J. (2010). *Early intervention for reading difficulties: The interactive strategies approach.* New York: Guilford Press.

Scarcella, R. (2003). *Academic English: A conceptual framework.* Irvine, CA: UC-LMRI.

Schoenfeld, A. (1992). Learning to think mathematically: problem solving, metacognition, and sense making in mathematics. In D. Grouws (Ed.), *Handbook of research in mathematics teaching and learning.* (pp. 334–370). New York: Macmillan Publishing Company.

Schoenfeld, A. (1987). What's all the fuss about metacognition? In A. Schoenfeld (Ed.), *Cognitive science and mathematics education* (p. 33–56). Hillsdale, NJ: Lawrence Erlbaum Associates.

Shores, C. & Chester, K. (2008). *Using RTI for school improvement: Raising every student's achievement.* Thousand Oaks, CA: Corwin Press.

Simmons, D. & Kame'enui, E. (1998). *What reading research tells us about children with diverse learning needs: Bases and basics.* New York, NY: Routledge.

Spillane, J. & Thompson, C. (1997). Reconstructing Conceptions of Local Capacity: The Local Education Agency's Capacity for Ambitious Instructional Reform. *Educational Evaluation and Policy Analysis, 19(2),* 185–203.

Smiley, P. & Salsberry, T. (2007). *Effective schooling for English language learners: What elementary principals should know and do.* Larchmont, NY: Eye On Education.

Snow, C. & Biancarosa, G. (2003). *Adolescent literacy and the achievement gap: What do we know and where do we go from here?* New York, NY: Carnegie Corporation.

Stahl, K. & Mckenna, M. (2006). *Reading research at work: Foundations of effective practice.* New York, NY: Guilford Press.

Stanley, J. (2009). *The rhetoric of remediation: Negotiating entitlement and access to higher education.* Pittsburgh, PA: University of Pittsburgh Press.

Stone, C., Silliman, E., Ehren, B., Appel, K. (2005). *Handbook of language and literacy: Development and disorders.* New York, NY: Guilford Press.

U.S. Department of Education (2009). State Policies on Procedures on Response to Intervention in the Midwest Region.

Valencia, S. & Buly, R. (2004). What struggling readers really need. *The Reading Teacher. 57,* 520–533.

Van de Walle, J. (2004). *Elementary and middle school mathematics: Teaching developmentally.* Boston, MA: Allyn & Bacon.

Webster, B. & Fisher, D. (2001). School-Level Environment and Student Outcomes in Mathematics Achievement. Paper presented at the Australian Association for Research in Education. December 3–6, 2001 Fremantle, Perth.

Weissbourd, R. (2009). *The parents we mean to be: How well-intentioned adults undermine children's moral and emotional development.* Boston, MA: Houghton Mifflin.

Wheeler, R. & Swords, R. (2006). *Code-switching: Teaching standard English in urban classrooms.* Urbana, IL: National Council of Teachers of English.

Wilms, J. (2003). Student Engagement at School—Sense of Belonging and Participation. Results from PISA 2000, Paris. Organisation for Economic Co-operation.

Winebrenner, S. (1996). *Teaching kids with learning difficulties in the regular classroom.* Minneapolis, MN: Free Spirit.

Wolfram, W., Adger, C. & Christian, D. (1999). *Dialects in schools and communities.* Mahwah, NJ: Lawrence Erlbaum Associates.

Notes